NO-FUSS COOKBOOK FOR NEWLYWEDS

NO-FUSS COOKBOOK FOR NEWLYWEDS

PRACTICAL TIPS AND PERFECTLY PORTIONED RECIPES TO COOK TOGETHER

RYAN ROSS

PHOTOGRAPHY BY PAUL SIRISALEE

ROCKRIDGE
PRESS

For general information on our other products and services or to obtain technical support, please contact our Customer Care Department within the U.S. at (866) 744-2665, or outside the U.S. at (510) 253-0500.

Rockridge Press publishes its books in a variety of electronic and print formats. Some content that appears in print may not be available in electronic books, and vice versa.

Interior and Cover Designer: Julie Schrader
Photo Art Director/Art Manager: Janice Ackerman
Editor: Bridget Fitzgerald
Production Editor: Ashley Polikoff
Photography: © 2020 Paul Sirisalee. Food styling by Kimberly Sirisalee.
Author Photo: Shawna Simmons and Nelina Loiselle ©The Scout Guide Hunt Country.
ISBN: Print 978-1-64611-415-3 | eBook 978-1-64611-416-0
R0

To Isla
Thank you for making our party of two a party of three.

TABLE OF CONTENTS

INTRODUCTION

I met my husband while riding the Q train in New York City. My opening line was "Are you heading to brunch, too?" As a chef living in New York City, I found my thoughts rarely veered very far from the subject of food. Was it even worth dating somebody who didn't feel the same way?

After a few years of dating, moving (first to Nicaragua, then to Washington State), and millions of breakfast tacos, it was a go. On Leap Day 2012, we hopped on a ferryboat in the San Juan Islands of the Pacific Northwest and promised to love, cherish, and cook together for as long as we both shall live . . . no matter the kitchen at hand.

As a professional chef, I haven't always had a fully stocked pantry or even a full-size refrigerator. I've done my share of cooking without electricity, catered events using toaster ovens, and often entertained guests sitting on pillows around a coffee table. Nevertheless, my sweetie and I were cooking together and having a ball—most of the time. It was sometimes hard to find recipes that didn't leave us with tons of leftovers or to create counter space when living in a one-room rental on a dairy farm or to carve out enough time to make breakfast, lunch, and dinner when living on an island that relied on a generator for power—and so our kitchen only had electricity a few hours a day. But here's the good news about what our experience taught us: No matter where we are, cooking for two is fun, and cooking together is even better.

From kitchen to kitchen, I've scribbled down our favorite recipes for two and come up with some time-saving hacks. I've also taken notes on how to maximize prep space—and share it—no matter the "kitch-sitch." I have scoured online listings for full-price kitchen appliances (but purchased most of them secondhand). I have also inherited some appliances and regifted the ones that do not serve us.

This book is a collection of all of these notes, hacks, and experiences. It is full of delicious, unfussy, fun, and always-forgiving recipes to make and enjoy together for everything from a dinner on the couch in front of the TV to a late-morning breakfast perched at the counter and a healthy weekend lunch. It also includes helpful information on how to stock your kitchen and which appliances are necessary (and which to leave off the registry), and, of course, lots of cooking tips and inspiration. I hope this book will not only help you build your own repertoire of tasty go-tos and favorites but also be a handy guide as you and your sweetie embark on your cooking adventures together.

We now have a house in Virginia (a whole house!), and though we may not need to store our small appliances in our car anymore, there is always a way to streamline. Whether it's cleaning out the spice rack or reorganizing the drawer full of storage containers, the goal is to make the kitchen an easy place to be, so that cooking is always something to look forward to, rather than an item on the chore wheel.

No matter where you are living in the world, cooking together is what makes a place feel like home. Sure, sometimes you'll just have a "you open the box and I'll stir in the cheese" sort of night, but it's still a meal shared, and it's valuable. A marriage and partnership centered around food is a happy one. Here's to you and the love of your life creating your own traditions in the kitchen, no matter the kitchen at hand.

CHAPTER 1

Your Kitchen Is a Disaster

The most important room in everybody's home is the kitchen. The place where everyone gathers and . . . gets in your way! The expression "too many cooks in the kitchen" isn't for nothing. Space can be limited, time can be critical, and dinner has to get on the table. Then there are the drawers that won't close, and *why* are there always a billion pot lids that don't seem to fit on any pots?

To further complicate matters, you might be cooking in a "cozy" (read: tiny) studio kitchen, or maybe you're renovating, or maybe your kitchen counter has become the graveyard for all of the small kitchen appliances that have piqued your interest over the years. Whatever the reason, it can sometimes be tough to find enough counter space to work, let alone for *both* of you to work. Don't worry: Whether you have a brand-new giant kitchen or just a camping fork between you, this chapter has you covered on how to set up your kitchen for two.

These guidelines will help you stay organized and stock up on the essentials so you can get on with making meals and memories together. Use these tips to clean out your cabinets, add to your registry or wish list, improve upon your existing cooking skills, or start from square one. Through this process, you'll learn how to share the kitchen with each other and create a mutual space where you can have some fun—and perhaps a cocktail—while cooking together.

Set Up for Success

If you're like me, you've lived with your partner well before you got hitched, and if you haven't starved to death, you must be doing something right. You might already have some basic equipment. Maybe you want to skip a registry or go ahead and return some of the nonsense that you put on there before you knew better (you really can pit and slice your own avocado; it builds character). The occasional functional flourish, like a pepper grinder, is very welcome, but a kitchen for two is truly about the basics.

Get the Basics

The first step is to get properly equipped. The following lists include the basic tools and equipment that are useful in just about every kitchen and helpful to cooks of all skill levels.

POTS AND PANS

A complete set of pots and pans with fitted lids is certainly nice to have, so sure, go ahead and let someone gift this to you or get it at a Black Friday sale. But all you really need when stocking a kitchen for two are a few versatile fundamentals. And when it comes to versatile, try to start out with skillets that are oven-safe, so you can start cooking on the stove and finish cooking in the oven. You'll want the following:

- Two skillets, one medium and one large, with lids.

- A medium saucepot with a lid. Think of a spaghetti pot.

- A small saucepot with a lid for quick jobs like heating up soup.

KNIVES

Here are the three basic blades to keep on hand:

A chef's knife or utility knife: This is the main knife you'll use for almost all of your chopping and slicing. It's important not to feel intimidated by your chef's knife, so go with a modest length and width. It's also helpful to test a few to see if you like the weight, length, and overall feel before you commit to a purchase. I mostly use a ceramic knife by Kyocera (see sidebar).

Serrated knife: A serrated knife is the only way to slice bread, bagels, baguettes, and other bread products neatly. It's also perfect for slicing tomatoes. Offset serrated knives are fairly inexpensive and cost around twenty dollars. They will need to be replaced once you notice the blade feels dull when slicing into a nice crusty bread boule.

Paring knife: Many folks make the mistake of using these small knives for big knife jobs. A paring knife has a short sharp blade that is only needed for precise jobs like peeling, cutting, or coring small fruits and vegetables.

KNIVES 101

Knives are made from many different materials. Here are my recommendations:

Ceramic: Ceramic blades can't be sharpened like metal blades, but they do keep their edge for years, which is a huge perk. They are lightweight, do not oxidize or discolor, and are great for fruit and vegetable butchering. They are the most cost effective and (bonus!) come in lots of fun colors.

Stainless steel: Stainless steel blades resist corrosion and staining due to the added element of chromium, which also makes stainless steel knives rust resistant. They won't oxidize or discolor when cutting citrus or purple cabbage, and they need very little maintenance. They will "lose their edge" much quicker, meaning that they do not stay sharp. Some stainless steel blades can be flimsy and would not be appropriate for tough jobs like cutting open a pumpkin or a butternut squash.

High-carbon steel: These blades keep a nice sharp edge and are tough and durable. High-carbon steel knives do require a bit of care; they should be kept dry and lightly oiled between uses so that they do not rust.

BAKEWARE

These basics will be all you need to start out:

Baking dish: A glass 9-by-13-by-2-inch dish can be used for a wide variety of recipes, including lasagna, casseroles, and brownies. You may also want a metal version for some baked goods, like cakes.

Baking sheets: Two or three rimmed 13-by-18-inch baking sheets are great for roasting vegetables and meats as well as making one-pan meals and cookies.

Dutch oven: These range in size and can hold anywhere from 1 to 14 quarts. When cooking for two, a 3-quart Dutch oven for stews and roasts is all you'll need.

Muffin pan: If you like muffins, you need a muffin pan. It is also convenient for making mini quiches, individual au gratins, filled puff pastries, and other similarly small or individually portioned items.

Nesting bowls: Having a variety of metal bowls is helpful when preparing meals big and small. Having bowls that fit snugly together will make storing them easier.

Springform pan: It is always nice to have a round baking dish, so you may as well buy one that's springform style, which has sides that are removable from the base (thereby saving you the trouble of inverting the pan and dealing with any potential sticking). These pans are great for cheesecakes, egg bakes, cakes, and breads.

SMALL TOOLS AND OTHER ITEMS
Here are my favorite go-to kitchen tools:

Box grater: This style of grater has a handle on top and four sides, each with a different grating size or pattern. It is good for shredding cheese, carrots, cabbage, and potatoes.

Citrus press: A handheld model can save the day when you need to squeeze a lemon or two and keep seeds out.

Cutting boards: I recommend keeping two on hand: A medium to large plastic one is easy to wash and can be sanitized easily after preparing meat and fish, and a small or medium wooden one is great for slicing fruits and vegetables. Having two also means you and your partner can slice and dice at the same time, if needed. Plastic is best to start with, since it's nonporous and dishwasher-safe.

Dish towels: You can never have enough kitchen towels.

Dry measuring cups: These cups usually come as a nested set with four sizes—1 cup, ½ cup, ⅓ cup, and ¼ cup—each with a long handle. They are used to measure dry ingredients like flour and sugar.

Liquid measuring cups: These cups are usually glass, with units marked on the side and a pour spout. A 2-cup liquid measuring cup will work for all of the recipes in this book. Common brands are Pyrex and Anchor.

Meat thermometer: This tool comes in handy for checking the doneness of your roasts and meats.

Offset spatula, aka pancake flipper: These spatulas have a little step-like bend near the handle-end of the paddle, making it easier to scoop up items for flipping (like pancakes).

Oven mitts: I like using square hot pads instead of oven mitts so I can grab things out of the oven quickly, rather than fussing with pulling on a glove.

Pepper grinder: Freshly ground black pepper is the only way to go.

Rubber spatula: Despite the name, these tools are mostly made of silicone these days. They are perfect for scraping down bowls of ingredients and using on nonstick pans.

Spiralizer: This small handheld tool makes "noodles" from zucchini, summer squash, sweet potatoes, and butternut squash.

Steamer basket: This perforated, collapsible metal basket can be dropped in any size pot or pan, with a bit of water in the bottom and a fitted lid on top, to steam vegetables in minutes. It's also easier to store than the larger 3- or 4-piece steamer pots.

Vegetable peeler: I like the Y-shape peelers. I find that they are sturdier and a more suitable shape for safely and efficiently peeling potatoes, butternut squash, and carrots.

Whisk: The tines, or wires, of a whisk are used to incorporate air into whatever you are whisking, making it light and fluffy. You can use a whisk to make fluffy scrambled eggs or to turn heavy cream into whipped cream.

Wooden spoon: This essential tool does everything and will last forever. Don't put it in the dishwasher!

Zester: When you need very finely grated lemon or orange peel, a zester is the perfect tool. You can also use it for grating hard cheeses (like Parmesan), ginger, and garlic.

Upgrade with Bonuses

Now that you have the basics down, here are some upgrades you can register for or put on your wish list for later.

Blender: Okay, so you don't need a blender with the engine of a speedboat, but blenders are so readily available now, why not get one of just slightly lesser power? It doesn't have to be a pricey Vitamix—I like models by Ninja, Blendtec, or NutriBullet.

Cast-iron skillet: The best way to obtain one of these skillets is to inherit one that has been treated well. We use one that belonged to my partner's grandmother. You need to season cast-iron pans, avoid washing them with soap, and keep them dry when not using them. Aside from being a bit high maintenance, they are awesome—they cook evenly, and you can use them on the stovetop, in the oven, and for serving.

Electric mixer or stand mixer: If someone is willing to gift you the wizard appliance that is the KitchenAid stand mixer, get thee to a YouTube channel to learn about all it can do! Pasta, ice cream, cakes, you name it. If you don't bake a ton, an electric handheld mixer will do just fine.

Food processor: Get a full-size processor if you have the space for it. It can be used to make soups, salsas, pesto, pastry crusts, nut butters, sauces, and more.

Glass storage containers: One of the worst things on Earth is an unruly drawer overflowing with mismatched plastic storage sets. Let Aunt Lydia single handedly save your marriage by gifting you some premium storage containers, like a set of glass Pyrex storage sets with fitted lids. Plus, they are oven-safe (though not the lids).

Salad spinner: Drying lettuce leaves off one-by-one is insane. Either buy the premixed, already-washed lettuce blends or get a salad spinner.

Upgraded wooden cutting board: A large butcher block–style cutting board will become the home base of your kitchen. It's a great piece you can keep on the counter full time.

Keep the Gift Receipts

Less is more in the kitchen. Free yourself from the gadgets that have only one use, such as a hard-boiled egg slicer, cherry pitter, or burger press. No one *needs* a fish-shaped water pitcher, a personal-size fondue fountain, three sets of salt and pepper shakers of different farm animals, or a rotisserie. Keep it simple, and you'll discover what you're missing as you go. (That said, if you've hosted fondue night weekly for three years, by all means, get those copper-handled retractable forks, and enjoy. Customizing a kitchen for two is all about doing what works for *you*.)

Change Up the Layout

Whether you are moving into a brand-new home, designing a full kitchen together, or living in your brother's finished basement that has something he calls a "kitchenette" (been there), the layout is important. You want to stream-line your space and create a kitchen that is functional for two cooks. This goal boils down to a few simple principles: Everything has a place, everything is accessible, and the kitchen is easy to clean.

The Work Triangle Is a Myth

News flash: We are not cookie-cutter people with cookie-cutter kitchens. The idea of the work triangle was birthed sometime around the 1940s, when kitchens were being designed with the stovetop, sink, and refrigerator situated for maximum efficiency and flow (in theory). In reality, the distance between these three appliances is moot—and most of us have little control over their placement, anyway.

What you want is counter space. This does not mean that you need yards of it or a giant island—just a space free from clutter and large enough to fit a cutting board (so it is easy to prep and lay out ingredients) and another space for clean dishes to dry (or where you can unload them from the dishwasher). Add a garbage can, compost, and recycling bin within easy reach, and you're good to go. (In a perfect world, these utility bins would be totally hands-free, so you aren't grubbing up your cabinets while you're mastering the art of cooking for two—or, you know, making hot dogs.)

Tailor for Two

Prime real estate in the kitchen may be a bit of a negotiation. Just as kitchens are not cookie cutter, neither are relationships. One of you may prioritize coffee as the very first thing upon waking, and the other may want a green smoothie. You can tailor your kitchen for two by creating space to dedicate toward each of your true loves—in this case, a coffee station with supplies readily at hand and a blender area ready to go each morning.

Try storing rarely used items, like the stand mixer or burner-hogging decorative teakettle, until you need them. If you seldom bake, free up that pantry space by storing all of your baking needs in a large bin with a lid—it doesn't even need to be in the kitchen if space is at a premium; try the garage or laundry room. Baking is like going camping; you need everything whether you are staying for one day or for five. So, having it all in one place is tidy and convenient.

The key to creating a comfortable and usable kitchen for two is to open up enough space to work without sacrificing the must-have homey touches that cater to your particular lifestyle—whether that's your French press or your prized juicer.

COCKTAIL PARTY FOR TWO—OR MORE

Starting the evening off with a cocktail is a great way to entertain guests—or each other. Doing so sets the tone for an awesome meal to come. One of you will soon discover that you are the house bartender, with that special knack for mixing up a boozy beverage for the two of you or for settling newly arrived guests with a libation.

Designate a place, away from the kitchen if possible (no need for extra bodies that aren't cooking), to store your wine, favorite spirit, a corkscrew and bottle opener, and any bar accoutrements you have. Free up a kitchen cabinet by adding a few floating shelves above the bar cart for storing your cocktail glasses and hanging your stemware.

Poof! You're now a mixologist, ready to entertain—and you've cleared some space in the cabinets, to boot.

Cooking for Two

Cooking for two can sometimes be more difficult than cooking for ten, mostly due to the twin issues of grocery shopping and leftovers. Grocery items don't always seem packaged to suit only two appetites, leaving you with a great deal of leftover spaghetti carbonara, hamburger buns, and the like.

Cooking for two, however, can help build bridges to things you wouldn't have otherwise tried, tasted, or cooked.

PROS	CONS
You don't have to cook for ten. Phew.	When you and your partner have differing tastes, it can lead to short-order cooking—one gets the grilled cheese, one gets the chili.
Bulk, or by-weight, sections were made for you. Measure out exactly how much rice, loose carrots, or honey you'll need at any given time.	Buying at big-box stores doesn't always make sense, even when it's "cheap." Sure, that case of 16 cartons of chicken stock is a great deal, but do you really need that many? No.
Practicing cooking together can lead to not only adventur-ous cooking but also adventurous eating. A sense of accomplishment comes from cooking meals for and with the ones you love. As you build confidence in the kitchen, you will want to expand your repertoire to include new dishes and flavors.	Too many leftovers. No one wants to eat the same lasagna for two weeks, no matter how tasty it is.
The industry is realizing the demand for smaller yields and recipes that don't automatically make 6 to 8 servings (see: this book!). More recipe availability means you always have some-thing new to try.	Cooking for two around the holidays is a bit overwhelming. You most likely don't need an entire turkey or want to do the prep work to only make two tamales, yet you still want to join in on the classic festivities. Try for-two recipes like Fondue for Two (page 74), or Roasted Chicken over Peasant Bread with Fingerlings (aka Million-Dollar Chicken; page 157).
A kitchen for two is better equipped to stay tidy and organized.	

Divide and Conquer

For each recipe in this book, there is a "Divide & Conquer" section that will divvy up the steps in each recipe between you and your partner. The more you cook together, the more you will see who is gravitating toward what, and you can either continue to grow in that direction or shake things up. For example, one of you can choose to chop (practice those knife skills!) instead of doing the cleanup, or vice versa.

Get It Together: Meal Planning

If meal planning is your thing, start with a little inspiration: Dog-ear or bookmark the recipes you want to try, then come up with a grocery list. Remember to check out your freezer, and go ahead and use that frozen chicken instead of buying more. Clean out your refrigerator before you shop, assessing what you already have on hand. This will save you money and time, and as a bonus, there will be plenty of room for the things you purchase when you return home with them.

Make sure you have enough containers, like reusable storage or zip-top bags, so when you get home from shopping you can wash and dry your lettuce and produce, making it easy to grab when a salad craving hits. You can even chop and store vegetables in preparation for the recipes you want to make later in the day or later in the week.

STRATEGIZING

If you and your partner can agree on your meals for the week ahead of time, you deserve a medal. Typically, I find that we love a few recipes dearly, so we keep those on a pretty solid rotation and then add something new to try. This not only keeps our weekly planning, shopping, and prepping for the week easy but also keeps us from getting into a Taco Tuesday-to-Thursday rut. Which, if I'm being honest, my partner would not mind too much.

SHOPPING

So, you're armed with your grocery bags and your list, and you're ready to shop. Start with the perimeter of the grocery store. Get your fresh produce, seafood, meat, and dairy. (These aren't always on the perimeter of every store, but it's a place to start.) Then you can cruise the labyrinth of the center aisles to get the pantry ingredients that you need. Don't forget the basics: Do you have enough salt at home? Olive oil? You'll need them.

PREPPING (FOR THE HIGHLY ORGANIZED)

Here's where I invoke the old adage "do as I say, not as I do." I can count on one hand how many times in my life I have actually batch-cooked on a Sunday for the entire week. But it is an awesome strategy if you can make it work for your schedule. Here's the version my partner and I have adopted: We take turns making a larger dish once a week, something like a stew, pasta, or a big batch of overnight oats, so there's always something fresh and homemade around when time doesn't allow for a full day of cooking intended to portion out the meals for the entire week. We aim to make our meals fresh together every day, and with our semi-batch cooking as our safety net, we never go hungry.

STOCK THE STAPLES

These are my favorite items that I like to stock up on or at least have one of each present in my pantry, refrigerator, or freezer at all times. Having a well-stocked assembly of basic and good ol' standby ingredients will encourage you to cook at home more often and will free up space from the previously prioritized packaged snacks and stacks of frozen pizzas.

Pantry

Apple cider vinegar: This vinegar provides a great balance to salty and sweet flavors in soups, dressings, and marinades.

Avocado oil (or coconut oil): For cooking, I prefer to use high-heat oil (any high-heat oil will do). These two are my go-tos.

Balsamic vinegar: A versatile and flavorful condiment, balsamic vinegar is great in marinades and dressings.

Honey: Honey can be packaged in both plastic squeeze bottles and glass jars. Bottles are easier to keep clean; if you purchase jarred honey, be sure to wipe the rim clean so the lid doesn't get sticky and become difficult to remove.

Maple syrup: This robust natural sweetener is perfect for sauces, dressings, and marinades, not to mention as a topping meant to be poured liberally over pancakes.

Olive oil: This delicate oil with a low smoke point is best for drizzling and for making dressings, not for heating.

Onions, garlic, and root vegetables: Vegetables such as sweet potatoes, yellow onions, red onions, and garlic last a long time and can be kept out on the counter in a bowl. Yellow, red, and Russet potatoes should be kept in a cool, dark place.

Nut or seed butter: Whether you prefer almond butter, peanut butter, or sunflower seed butter, crunchy or smooth, get your favorite. I have written the recipes so that nut and seed butters are, for the most part, interchangeable in these recipes.

Peppercorns: Look for whole black peppercorns to fill your pepper mill, or pick up one that has its own grinder. The flavor of freshly ground black pepper is so much better than pre-ground pepper.

Salt: I recommend fine-grain sea salt, like Himalayan, or kosher salt, if you prefer it.

Spices and dried herbs: You'll want to have spices like powdered cinnamon, chili powder, and cumin on hand. I also recommend dried herb blends like herbes de Provence and an Italian blend.

Thai curry paste: A little jar goes a long way. I like the red and green curry pastes by Thai Kitchen.

Refrigerator

Apples: Apples are the original grab-and-go snack, and they're also great to have on hand for impromptu dessert making.

Arugula: This delicious bitter green can be the base of a salad or tossed on top of most savory dishes for a little color.

Butter: I stick to salted butter because . . . I love salt. But the general rule is if you use salted butter, add a smaller pinch of salt when you are seasoning your dish, and if you use unsalted butter, add a larger pinch. Otherwise, it's largely personal preference.

Dijon mustard: This mainstay is the secret ingredient to most sauces, marinades, and salad dressings.

Eggs: Eggs are quick and easy protein for breakfast or a snack, and they don't go bad quickly. Stock up.

Ketchup: Good on everything, amirite? I use it as a base for barbecue sauce, in meatballs, and in meat loaf.

Lemons: They look pretty on the counter, but they store best in the refrigerator.

Mayonnaise: Look for high-quality brands like Duke's, Sir Kensington's, or Primal Kitchen avocado oil mayonnaise.

Spinach: Spinach is the easiest green vegetable to add almost anywhere for extra nutrition.

Tamari: Tamari is a Japanese sauce that is basically a gluten-free soy sauce.

Freezer

Bananas: When your bananas start getting pretty freckled and edging toward being overripe, pop them in the freezer so you can use them when you're ready. Frozen ripe bananas are great for quick smoothies.

Berries: Keep a small assortment of frozen berries on hand for smoothies, baked goods, and simple desserts like a quick crisp.

Butter: Before you know it, you will be out of butter, and you will thank yourself for always having a pound in the freezer.

Chicken thighs: Bone-in and skin-on chicken thighs are a great go-to when cooking for two. The packaged four-packs (1 to 2 pounds) are spot on, and you can dress them up with lots of different flavors.

Frozen pizza: For good measure.

Ground beef: When you are low on time or feel like making something easy, keep some ground beef on hand for burgers, meatballs, or meat loaf.

Shrimp: Frozen peeled and deveined shrimp cooks quickly and is an easy go-to on nights when you're short on time.

Soup: It's never a bad idea to have homemade soup at the ready.

Steaks: Steaks are perfect to keep handy for a grill night, but don't forget to pull them out of the freezer the night before.

Stock: Keep some frozen stock on hand for cooking grains, like rice, and for soups.

Whole chicken: If you can remember to move it into the refrigerator and thaw it the night before, it's great to have one on hand for roast chicken dinners or to add any pulled leftovers to soups, sandwiches, and salads.

About the Recipes

Cooking for two is about having fun and not being totally rigid about measuring or getting everything exactly right. These recipes are created from my own experience of cooking for two. Some recipes I learned from my husband while we were dating, others I created while experimenting in the kitchen, some were happy accidents, and still others were passed down from friends and family. They are all designed to be user friendly and forgiving.

What's for Dinner?

All cooks are welcome here. Use this book as a manual to help whittle down your choices for meals to make together. Check out the labels on each recipe to help you decide. If you're craving comfort food, look for the Comfort Food label and try Chicken Paprikash on page 155. How about an impromptu date night? You'll find Lamb on a Stick with Wilted Spinach on page 85 using the label Date Night. The labels also note dietary restrictions and preferences, like Gluten-Free, Vegetarian, and Nut-Free. There is something here for everyone.

Coming home late from work? Check out the chapter on 30-minute meals, and make Chili-Lime Shrimp Salad on page 70. Haven't grocery shopped in a month? Look up one of the five-ingredient recipes in chapter 4—you might just have everything you need in the freezer and pantry for something like Panfried Chicken with Hot Honey (page 114). All of the recipes in this chapter have five ingredients or fewer (not counting salt, pepper, butter, or oil).

You can also thumb through What's for Dinner? (page 186) to find recipes that match what you have on hand or what you are in the mood for—maybe you're craving something with bacon or want to try a new side dish. You'll find lists for these and more at the end of the book.

Tips, Labels, and Ingredients

You won't need to skim the ingredient lists of twenty recipes in order to find a nut-free or vegetarian one; every recipe is labeled with dietary specifics and cross-referenced in the index (page 194) for easy-breezy recipe searching. (Please remember, for all recipes in this book that are gluten free, always check ingredient packaging for gluten-free labeling before purchasing in order to ensure foods, especially oats, were processed in a completely gluten-free facility.)

All recipes will also include tips and tricks that include all my favorite little tidbits and hacks to make cooking from this book simple, fast, and fun. Here are the types of tips you will find in the recipes.

Kitchen hack: a creative solution to something that is otherwise complicated

Prep tip: suggestions on how to make meal prep, cooking, and cleanup easier

Cooking 101: basic cooking lessons and helpful clarification of cooking methods

Swap it out: suggestions for subbing out ingredients in order to try something new or for a different flavor profile

Ingredient tip: helpful knowledge about how to pick out ingredients like produce or where one may find something like tahini in your local grocery store, plus nutritional information and interesting food facts

Mix it up: fun and simple ways to amp up your recipe, if you are feeling fancy, by adding ingredients

*Savory Peach and Melon
Gazpacho with Feta, page 30*

CHAPTER 2

No-Cook

Cinnamon, Apple, and Almond Butter Overnight Oats

DAIRY-FREE, GLUTEN-FREE OPTION, VEGAN

Serves 2 / Prep time: 10 minutes, plus overnight to chill

We love overnight oats in our house because they taste great and are easy to make, and you can easily change the ingredients for endless variation. If you have pears or berries, use those; if you have leftover apple crisp, add it in! Overnight oats are a great snack to have on hand when you just need a quick bite of something to tide you over. Portion this recipe into mason jars with fitted lids for an easy breakfast or snack to go. They keep in the refrigerator for 4 to 5 days.

1½ cups rolled oats (or gluten-free rolled oats)

2 cups almond milk

½ cup almond butter

¼ cup maple syrup

1 teaspoon ground cinnamon

1 teaspoon vanilla extract

½ teaspoon salt

1 cup chopped apple

¼ cup chopped walnuts

1. Put the oats in a medium mixing bowl, and cover them with the almond milk. Stir to make sure all of the oats get saturated.

2. Stir in the almond butter, creating a swirl throughout the oats. Add the maple syrup, cinnamon, vanilla, and salt. Mix well.

3. Sprinkle in the apple and walnuts. Stir to evenly distribute all the ingredients throughout the oat mixture.

4. Divide the overnight oats between two 8-ounce jars with fitted lids, or simply cover the bowl with plastic wrap. Refrigerate for 6 to 8 hours or overnight.

Mix it up: The list of possible ingredients for overnight oats is endless. Some more of my favorite items to rotate in are bananas, blueberries, chia seeds, chocolate chips, hempseed, honey, peanut butter, pumpkin seeds, and sunflower seed butter.

Per Serving Calories: 910; Total Fat: 52g; Saturated Fat: 4g; Sodium: 743mg; Carbohydrates: 100g; Fiber: 16g; Sugars: 42g; Protein: 20g

DIVIDE & CONQUER:
Partner 1 can chop the apple and walnuts while partner 2 completes steps 1 and 2.

Chocolate Chia Pudding Pots

DAIRY-FREE, GLUTEN-FREE, VEGAN

Serves 2 / Prep time: 5 minutes, plus 1 hour to chill

Chia pudding has been a rising star in the last few years because it's a healthy excuse for having dessert for breakfast. This pudding is super-nutritious and a great alternative to plain old yogurt for breakfast. There are so many wonderful flavor options for this dish. You can try peaches and cinnamon if chocolate isn't doing it for you—or make a batch of each, because hey, it's that easy.

1½ tablespoons unsweetened cocoa

3 tablespoons maple syrup

¼ teaspoon salt

1 cup coconut milk

¼ cup chia seeds

Raspberries, chocolate chips, or sliced bananas, for topping (optional)

1. Using a flour sifter or a fine-mesh sieve, sift the cocoa powder into a small mixing bowl so there are no clumps. Add the maple syrup and salt, then whisk while pouring in the coconut milk little by little to make a cocoa paste. Continue until all of the coconut milk is incorporated.

2. Whisk in the chia seeds until combined. Divide the chia mixture between two jars or cups. Cover, and refrigerate for at least 1 hour.

3. When you are ready to serve the pudding, top each serving with raspberries, chocolate chips, or bananas (if using). The pudding will keep for 4 to 5 days in the refrigerator.

Ingredient tip: Don't be fooled by the tiny size of the chia seed. These superseeds pack a powerful punch and are seriously nutritious. They are loaded with omega-3 fatty acids, fiber, protein, and various micronutrients.

Per Serving Calories: 420; Total Fat: 28g; Saturated Fat: 19g; Sodium: 325mg; Carbohydrates: 35g; Fiber: 11g; Sugars: 20g; Protein: 8g

DIVIDE & CONQUER:

Partner 1 can sift while partner 2 measures and adds the maple syrup. Then partner 1 can continue whisking as partner 2 gradually pours in the coconut milk. Partner 1 can whisk in the chia seeds while partner 2 gets out the jars.

Chocolate-Cherry Granola Bars

DAIRY-FREE, GLUTEN-FREE OPTION, VEGAN

Makes 6 bars / Prep time: 5 minutes, plus 1 hour to chill

There are plenty of packaged bars on the market these days, but nothing tastes better than homemade. This recipe is also very forgiving—after the first few times you make it, you probably won't need to measure the ingredients at all—and with an extra spoonful of chocolate chips here or an extra pinch of salt there, this recipe will eventually become your own.

1 cup rolled oats (or gluten-free rolled oats)

¼ cup pumpkin seeds

¼ cup dried cherries

¼ cup mini chocolate chips

1 tablespoon unsweetened cocoa powder

¼ teaspoon salt

¼ cup peanut butter

¼ cup maple syrup

½ teaspoon vanilla extract

1. Line a 9-by-13-inch baking dish with parchment paper.

2. In a medium mixing bowl, stir together the oats, pumpkin seeds, dried cherries, chocolate chips, cocoa powder, and salt until well combined.

3. Using a wooden spoon or your clean hands, mix in the peanut butter, maple syrup, and vanilla. Continue to mix everything together until the mixture forms a sticky dough that will stay together when pinched or rolled into a ball.

4. Transfer the sticky dough to the prepared baking dish, and press the oat mixture into an even layer. Cover with plastic wrap, and refrigerate for at least 1 hour.

5. Cut into six roughly 3-by-6½-inch bars (or into the size and shape you prefer), and serve. Store in an airtight container for up to 1 week.

Mix it up: To make these bars extra fancy, you can melt a small amount of chocolate and drizzle it on top before chilling.

Per Serving (1 bar) Calories: 245; Total Fat: 12g; Saturated Fat: 3g; Sodium: 166mg; Carbohydrates: 31g; Fiber: 3g; Sugars: 18g; Protein: 7g

---

DIVIDE & CONQUER:
Partner 1 can complete step 1 and measure out the peanut butter, maple syrup, and vanilla while partner 2 completes step 2.

Whipped Feta and Spiced Honey Schmear

NUT-FREE, VEGETARIAN

Serves 4 / Prep time: 15 minutes

A quick crostini recipe is a shortcut to an elegant appetizer or, if you have a few, makes for a nice, light meal paired with soup or salad. Whipped feta has become a pretty common condiment in my house—other than spreading it on toast, we will also top fish or chicken with a dollop or use it straight up as a dip for chips, cucumbers, and sliced red bell peppers. Whipped feta will store in the refrigerator for about 1 week in a container with a tight-fitting lid.

8 ounces feta cheese

2 ounces cream cheese

2 tablespoons olive oil

Pinch ground cinnamon

Pinch ground cloves

Pinch chipotle
   chile powder

2 to 4 hearty bread or
   baguette slices

1 tablespoon honey

1. Crumble the feta cheese, and let it come to room temperature, about 8 minutes.

2. Put the feta in a food processor, and pulse a few times until finely crumbled. Add the cream cheese and olive oil. Pulse for 3 to 4 minutes, or until very smooth.

3. In a small mixing bowl, mix together the cinnamon, cloves, and chile powder.

4. Toast the bread.

5. Smear each piece of bread with a thick layer of the whipped feta, drizzle the honey on top, and finish with a big pinch of the spice blend.

Mix it up: Try topping these crostini with tomatoes, berries, roasted pears, or roasted pumpkin.

Per Serving Calories: 364; Total Fat: 25g; Saturated Fat: 12g; Sodium: 860mg; Carbohydrates: 21g; Fiber: 1g; Sugars: 8g; Protein: 12g

---

DIVIDE & CONQUER:

Partner 1 can process the whipped feta in steps 1 and 2 while partner 2 tackles steps 3 and 4.

Savory Peach and Melon Gazpacho with Feta

GLUTEN-FREE, NUT-FREE, VEGETARIAN, VEGAN OPTION

Serves 2 / Prep time: 10 minutes

This delightful, no-cook soup is the best balance of sweet, juicy, spicy, and salty. It is also a great way to use up a huge honking melon that is taking up all of the room in your refrigerator. Try this recipe out on a warm day for lunch or for entertaining guests as a first course. Since most of these ingredients will be going into a food processor, there's no need to labor over perfectly diced watermelon or tomatoes; just break down the items into manageable chunks, 1 inch or so, in order to fit them into your food processor bowl.

1 peach, peeled, pitted, and cut into chunks

1 cup watermelon chunks

½ cup tomato chunks

½ cup cucumber chunks

2 tablespoons chopped red onion

1 teaspoon minced jalapeño pepper

1 teaspoon minced garlic

½ teaspoon salt, plus more as needed

5 fresh mint leaves

5 fresh basil leaves

1 tablespoon honey (or maple syrup)

1. Put the peach, watermelon, tomato, cucumber, and onion in a food processor. Pulse until all of the ingredients are finely chopped and have released their juices. Scrape down the sides of the food processor bowl with a rubber spatula in between pulses, if needed.

2. Add the jalapeño pepper, garlic, salt, mint, basil, honey, and lime juice. Run the food processor while drizzling in the olive oil. Taste the gazpacho and season with more salt, if needed.

3. Serve the gazpacho with the feta (if using) and a few turns of freshly ground black pepper.

1 tablespoon freshly
squeezed lime juice
¼ cup olive oil
2 tablespoons crum-
bled feta cheese
(optional)
Freshly ground
black pepper

Ingredient tip: Capsaicin, which can be found in the seeds of chile peppers, can cause burning or itching sensations on the skin. You can adjust the heat of your gazpacho by removing or adding the jalapeño seeds. Always wash your hands thoroughly after handling chile peppers of any kind, or wear gloves when you are handling them.

Per Serving Calories: 337; Total Fat: 28g; Saturated Fat: 4g; Sodium: 588mg; Carbohydrates: 24g; Fiber: 2g; Sugars: 20g; Protein: 2g

---

DIVIDE & CONQUER:

Partner 1 can work on breaking down the peach, melon, tomato, cucumber, and onion and pulsing them in the food processor while partner 2 carefully chops the jalapeño pepper, washing their hands very well afterward, or better yet, using gloves.

Dill Cucumber Noodles with Smoked Salmon

GLUTEN-FREE, NUT-FREE

Serves 2 / Prep time: 10 minutes

If you have a spiralizer, you may know your way around zucchini "noodles," but why not try cucumber on for a crunchy change? This salad dish will not keep very well due to the water content of the cucumber and the salt that will continue to leech liquid as the dish sits, so only "zoodle" as much cucumber as you would like to eat in one sitting.

2 cucumbers

2 teaspoons freshly
    squeezed
    lemon juice

1 teaspoon
    Dijon mustard

2 tablespoons minced
    red onion

1 tablespoon olive oil

¼ teaspoon salt

2 ounces
    smoked salmon

2 tablespoons
    sour cream

1 tablespoon chopped
    fresh dill

1 tablespoon capers
    (optional)

Freshly ground
    black pepper

1. Spiralize the cucumbers into a medium mixing bowl. (If you do not have a spiralizer to make the cucumber noodles, use a vegetable peeler to peel long ribbons out of the skin and flesh of the cucumber until you get to the seedy center. Discard the seeds. Put the noodles in a medium mixing bowl.)

2. In a small mixing bowl, whisk together the lemon juice, mustard, and onion while drizzling in the olive oil. Add the salt and whisk again. Pour the dressing over the noodles, and toss until well coated.

3. Top the noodles with the salmon, sour cream, dill, and capers (if using). Serve with several turns of freshly ground black pepper.

Prep tip: If you love red onion like I do, feel free to add onion to this recipe. If you have a mandoline, you can use it to make paper-thin slices of onion, which are perfect for not only this dish but also any dish that includes raw onion. Paper-thin is the way to go, and a mandoline is the best way to get there.

Per Serving Calories: 169; Total Fat: 11g; Saturated Fat: 3g; Sodium: 930mg; Carbohydrates: 10g; Fiber: 3g; Sugars: 7g; Protein: 8g

DIVIDE & CONQUER:
Partner 1 can make the cucumber "noodles" and measure out the salmon, sour cream, and capers while partner 2 handles the dressing.

Crunchy Thai-Style Veggie Noodle Salad with Peanut Sauce

DAIRY-FREE, GLUTEN-FREE, VEGETARIAN, VEGAN OPTION

Serves 2 / Prep time: 15 minutes

. . . .

This recipe is a lighter take on takeout. I love peanut sauce on just about everything, and this dish combines all of my favorite things in the rich, umami-laden, peanutty dressing. These veggie "noodles" are a great alternative to grain pasta and a fun way to change up your lunch or light dinner.

For the peanut sauce

Zest and juice of 1 lime
1 tablespoon honey (or maple syrup)
2 tablespoons peanut butter
2 tablespoons tamari
1 teaspoon sriracha
1 teaspoon minced garlic
1 teaspoon minced ginger
¼ cup sesame oil

For the noodles

¼ small red cabbage, thinly sliced or shredded into long ribbons
¼ small green cabbage, thinly sliced or shredded into long ribbons
¼ red onion, thinly sliced
1 red bell pepper, thinly sliced

To make the peanut sauce

1. In a blender, pulse together the lime zest and juice, honey, peanut butter, tamari, sriracha, garlic, and ginger while streaming in the sesame oil. Blend in up to 2 tablespoons of water if the sauce is too thick.

To make the noodles

2. In a large mixing bowl, combine the red cabbage, green cabbage, onion, bell pepper, and radishes.

3. Spiralize the carrots, cucumber, and zucchini. (If you do not have a spiralizer, use a vegetable peeler to create "noodles" down the length of the vegetables, rotating each one as it is being peeled until you reach the core. Discard the core.) Add the "noodles," bean sprouts, and mango (if using) to the other vegetables in the bowl.

4. Pour the sauce over the veggie noodles, and toss to combine. Top with the basil, mint, cilantro, and peanuts.

2 small radishes,
   thinly sliced

2 carrots

1 cucumber

1 zucchini

½ cup bean sprouts

1 small mango, cut
   into matchsticks
   (optional)

5 fresh basil leaves, torn

5 fresh mint leaves, torn

½ bunch fresh cilantro,
   leaves picked

¼ cup crushed peanuts

Swap it out: If you happen to spot Thai basil in your local grocery store, try swapping it in for traditional basil. Thai basil has an unmistakable flavor, with a hint of licorice, and will make this dish really sing.

Per Serving Calories: 610; Total Fat: 46g; Saturated Fat: 7g; Sodium: 1,239mg; Carbohydrates: 41g; Fiber: 14g; Sugars: 20g; Protein: 18g

---

DIVIDE & CONQUER:
Partner 1 can get to work on chopping and slicing all the vegetables while partner 2 blends the peanut sauce.

Peach, Prosciutto, Rocket, and Burrata Salad

DATE NIGHT, GLUTEN-FREE, NUT-FREE

Serves 2 / Prep time: 10 minutes

Tomato, basil, and mozzarella. The trio that makes up the traditional Caprese salad is close to my heart, but the combination in this salad might just have it beat. Burrata is a young mozzarella that has a luxurious softer center. Paired with sweet peach, salty prosciutto, the slightly bitter bite of arugula—or the more fun "rocket," as they call it in the United Kingdom—and topped with a tangy sweet drizzle of the balsamic vinegar and honey, it makes for a salad that has made me fall in love all over again.

2 cups loosely
    packed arugula
Juice of ½ lemon
2 teaspoons olive oil
Salt
Freshly ground
    black pepper
2 peaches
8 strips prosciutto
2 balls burrata cheese
1 tablespoon bal-
    samic vinegar
2 teaspoons honey

1. In a medium mixing bowl, dress the arugula with the lemon juice and olive oil. Season with salt and pepper. Toss, and arrange on a serving plate or in a serving bowl.

2. Cut each peach into 8 wedges, and place on top of the arugula. Tear the prosciutto, and arrange it among the arugula and peaches.

3. Top the salad with the burrata. Season the burrata generously with salt and pepper, then drizzle the entire salad with the vinegar and honey and serve family style.

Swap it out: If you can't find ripe peaches, you can try nectarines, cantaloupe, or even blackberries or cherries in this dish.

Per Serving Calories: 455; Total Fat: 31g; Saturated Fat: 5g; Sodium: 433mg; Carbohydrates: 21g; Fiber: 2g; Sugars: 15g; Protein: 24g

DIVIDE & CONQUER:

Partner 1 can complete step 1 while partner 2 slices the peaches, tears the prosciutto, and unpacks the burrata.

Broccoli, Tart Cherry, and Pecan Slaw with Poppy Seed Dressing

DAIRY-FREE, GLUTEN-FREE, VEGETARIAN

Serves 4 / Prep time: 20 minutes

It has always been such a shame to me to see the tough and woody stalks of broccoli go straight into the compost or rubbish bin. This slaw is the lifeline to broccoli stalks everywhere looking for a shot. Broccoli slaw is a great side for sandwiches, baked fish, or fried chicken. Not a pecan fan? Try pumpkin seeds or sunflower seeds instead.

For the slaw

1 head broccoli
½ cup chopped pecans
¼ cup dried tart cherries
¼ red onion,
    finely chopped

For the dressing

1 tablespoon
    mayonnaise
1 teaspoon
    Dijon mustard
2 teaspoons honey
1 tablespoon cham-
    pagne vinegar
1 teaspoon poppy seeds
Salt
Freshly ground
    black pepper

To make the slaw

1. Chop the broccoli tops off, setting the broccoli stalks aside. Rough chop the florets until they are tiny, no bigger than bite size. Scrape them into a medium mixing bowl.

2. Slice or peel away the woody exterior to the broccoli stalks, and discard. Using a box grater, grate the stalks into the bowl with the chopped florets.

3. Put the pecans in a small dry skillet over medium heat. Toast them for 2 to 3 minutes, stirring constantly, or until they give off a toasty, nutty aroma.

4. Add the pecans, cherries, and onion to the bowl, and mix well.

continued >>

To make the dressing

5. In a small mixing bowl, whisk the mayonnaise to remove any lumps. Add the mustard and honey and continue to whisk as you add the vinegar and poppy seeds. Season with a few pinches of salt and several turns of freshly ground black pepper.

6. Dress the broccoli slaw, and toss until well coated.

Mix it up: Try grating in carrot for more veg and color.

Per Serving Calories: 218; Total Fat: 15g; Saturated Fat: 1g; Sodium: 92mg; Carbohydrates: 21g; Fiber: 6g; Sugars: 12g; Protein: 6g

**DIVIDE &
CONQUER:**
Partner 1 can start with breaking down the broccoli into florets and grating the stalks while partner 2 toasts the pecans and makes the dressing.

Cilantro-Lime Cabbage Slaw with Ginger-Cashew Dressing

DAIRY-FREE, GLUTEN-FREE, VEGETARIAN, VEGAN OPTION

Serves 4 / Prep time: 10 minutes

I love a good traditional slaw, but after experimenting with the flavor profiles of tamari (a thicker, less salty, typically wheat-free soy sauce) and lime, along with the creaminess of the cashew, I crown this slaw as king. My partner and I eat this with salmon, with crab cakes—heck, we even eat it alongside scrambled eggs. Include as many crunchy additions as you see fit: crushed smoked almonds, cucumbers, red cabbage for some color, sprouts, you name it.

1 head napa cabbage, thinly sliced

¼ red onion, thinly sliced

2 radishes, thinly sliced

1 carrot, grated

½ cup loosely packed fresh cilantro leaves

¼ cup cashews

1 tablespoon minced fresh ginger

2 tablespoons tamari

1 tablespoon honey (or maple syrup)

2 tablespoons sesame oil

Zest and juice of 1 lime

2 tablespoons water

1. Put the cabbage, onion, radishes, carrot, and cilantro in a medium mixing bowl.

2. Put the cashews, ginger, tamari, honey, sesame oil, and lime zest and juice in a blender. Blend while pouring in the water a tablespoon at a time to create a creamy and smooth dressing.

3. Spoon the dressing over the slaw, and toss to coat all the vegetables very well.

continued >>

Kitchen hack: While holding fresh herbs by the stems with one hand, like a bouquet, lay them onto a cutting board with the leaves facing away from you. Use a knife in the other hand to cut at an angle, away from your body, almost like you are shaving or whittling the leaves away from the stems. Now you can pick though and remove the larger pieces of stems left in the pile. Beats picking leaves off one by one.

Per Serving Calories: 166; Total Fat: 11g; Saturated Fat: 2g; Sodium: 592mg; Carbohydrates: 14g; Fiber: 1g; Sugars: 6g; Protein: 5g

DIVIDE & CONQUER:
Partner 1 can slice and grate the vegetables for the slaw while partner 2 makes the dressing.

Nutella and Strawberry Fool

GLUTEN-FREE, VEGETARIAN

Serves 4 / **Prep time:** 15 minutes

If you like whipped cream and if you like pudding, this recipe will be a home run. We started enjoying fruit fools in this house when we were crawling the walls for a dessert one night and all that we had on hand that could possibly resemble a treat were some frozen blueberries and heavy cream. I whipped the cream, folded in the berries, and claimed to be a genius. But it was quickly pointed out that I was actually making a "fool" . . . of myself. A fruit fool is a traditional English dessert made by whipping cream and folding in fruit, jam, chocolate, and the like. No matter who started it, a fool will certainly scratch the dessert itch when your cupboards are nearly bare.

For the berry sauce

2 cups fresh strawber-
   ries, stemmed and
   quartered
1 tablespoon sugar
1 tablespoon
   freshly squeezed
   lemon juice
½ teaspoon
   vanilla extract

For the cream

1½ cups heavy cream
¼ cup powdered sugar
½ cup Nutella

To make the berry sauce

1. In a medium mixing bowl, toss the strawberries with the sugar, lemon juice, and vanilla. Allow them to sit for 5 minutes to macerate, letting the juices release from the berries.

2. Transfer half of the berry mixture to a blender, and blend until smooth. Pour the blended berries over the quartered berries, and stir.

To make the cream

3. Using a whisk, hand mixer, or stand mixer, whip together the cream and powdered sugar until thick and fluffy. (It is ready when you pull out the whisk and a firm peak forms.)

continued »

4. Spoon the Nutella into the cream. Using a rubber spatula, gently combine until the Nutella looks like ribbons throughout the cream.

5. Add the berry sauce, and fold in the same manner as you did with the Nutella.

6. Divide among 4 serving dishes, then cover and refrigerate until ready to serve.

Kitchen hack: Very cold cream and a cold bowl will help you whip the cream faster, so pop your mixing bowl in the refrigerator until you are ready to whip.

Per Serving Calories: 573; Total Fat: 44g; Saturated Fat: 24g; Sodium: 51mg; Carbohydrates: 41g; Fiber: 3g; Sugars: 38g; Protein: 5g

> **DIVIDE & CONQUER:**
> *Partner 1 can start with stemming, slicing, and macerating the berries while partner 2 whips the cream. Partner 1 can spoon in the Nutella and berries while partner 2 folds them in.*

Probably Your Grandmother's Cookies and Cream Icebox Cake

DATE NIGHT, NUT-FREE, VEGETARIAN

Makes 6 mini cakes / Prep time: 15 minutes, plus 3 hours to chill

How old is this recipe, you ask? It's from back when the refrigerator was called an icebox, and it's an often forgotten and underappreciated gem in my book. The unmatched goodness of chocolate and vanilla is a classic to which I am truly devout. However, in the summer months, it is fun to change up this recipe by using graham crackers instead of chocolate wafer cookies and adding fresh strawberry slices to the layers. Keeping the cakes tiny and in individually sized portions makes the chill time shorter. If you are making a bigger version of this cake, it will take overnight to soften the wafer cookie layers.

4 cups heavy cream

⅓ cup powdered sugar

1 teaspoon
    vanilla extract

Pinch salt

1 (9-ounce) package
    chocolate wafer cook-
    ies, such as Famous
    Chocolate Wafers

Fresh raspberries, for
    topping (optional)

Chocolate shavings, for
    topping (optional)

1. In a large mixing bowl, combine the cream, sugar, vanilla, and salt. Using a whisk, hand mixer, or stand mixer, whip until the cream is thick and fluffy. (It is ready when you pull out the whisk and a firm peak forms.)

2. Line a baking sheet with parchment paper. Lay out 6 wafer cookies on the prepared baking sheet, and spoon 1 heaping tablespoon of cream on top of each. Top each with another wafer cookie. Repeat this process 3 more times, ending with a wafer cookie on top.

3. Using the rest of the whipped cream, frost the outside of each stack. Top with berries (if using) or chocolate shavings (if using).

continued >>

4. Refrigerate for at least 3 hours, then serve.

Kitchen hack: Make curled chocolate shavings by running a vegetable peeler along the edges of a bar of chocolate, then sprinkle on top of the icebox cake.

Per Serving (1 mini cake) Calories: 762; Total Fat: 65g; Saturated Fat: 39g; Sodium: 367mg; Carbohydrates: 43g; Fiber: 1g; Sugars: 25g; Protein: 6g

DIVIDE & CONQUER:
Partner 1 can whip the cream (step 1) while partner 2 lines the baking sheet and lays out the wafer cookies. Partner 1 can scoop on the cream while partner 2 stacks the wafers.

Sweet Balsamic Berries and Vanilla Bean Cream

GLUTEN-FREE, NUT-FREE, VEGETARIAN

Serves 2 / Prep time: 15 minutes

I love when desserts sound fancy enough to require a dessert menu, but in reality, a monkey could do this one. This is a quick and elegant sweet to have if you are looking to make your casual night in a wee bit more special. The leftovers are also fantastic the next morning on waffles or pancakes.

For the berries

¼ cup balsamic vinegar
2 tablespoons honey
2 cups fresh berries (a mix of raspberries, blueberries, black-berries, and sliced strawberries)

For the cream

1 cup heavy cream
Paste from 1 vanilla bean (see Cooking 101)
1 tablespoon honey, plus more for drizzling
Pinch flake salt
Fresh mint leaves, poppy seeds, or grated lemon zest, for garnish (optional)

To make the berries

1. In a small mixing bowl, whisk together the vinegar and honey.

2. Rinse the berries, shake off the excess water, and put them into a medium mixing bowl.

3. Pour the balsamic honey mixture over the berries and stir. Allow them to sit for at least 10 minutes to macerate, stirring periodically to help release the juices from the berries.

To make the cream

4. If whipping the cream by hand, use a whisk and make lofty and vigorous stirring motions from the wrist to beat air into the cream. You can also use a hand mixer or stand mixer.

5. When the cream has thickened to the point where soft peaks form as you lift out the whisk, add the vanilla bean paste, honey, and salt. Resume whisking until firm peaks form. Be careful not to overwhip, or you will be on your way to making butter.

continued >>

SWEET BALSAMIC BERRIES AND VANILLA BEAN CREAM *continued*

6. Divide the berries between two small serving bowls and top with a generous amount of cream.

7. Garnish with another drizzle of honey, as well as mint leaves, poppy seeds, or lemon zest, if you'd like.

Cooking 101: To split your vanilla bean, use the tip of a paring knife and slice through the long pod lengthwise, then using the edge of your knife, scrape out the black speckled paste from within. But don't throw away that spent vanilla bean pod. Add it to a cup of sugar and let sit for a few days, or like, forever, and then you'll have vanilla sugar. Great in desserts, coffee, etc.

Per Serving Calories: 583; Total Fat: 45g; Saturated Fat: 27g; Sodium: 96mg; Carbohydrates: 47g; Fiber: 6g; Sugars: 36g; Protein: 4g

DIVIDE & CONQUER: *Partner 1 can take on the berries while partner 2 warms up their wrist and gets to whipping that cream! (You can, of course, also use a hand mixer or stand mixer.)*

Frozen Blueberry Cream Tart

DAIRY-FREE, GLUTEN-FREE, VEGAN

Makes 1 (8-inch) tart (about 8 slices) / Prep time: 20 minutes, plus overnight to soak the cashews and 6 to 8 hours to chill the tart

At a glance, this dessert could easily pass for cheesecake. The cashew cream base has the look and texture of thick, creamy cheesecake filling and takes on the complementary flavors of the berries, chocolate, lemon, or whatever you decide to pair with it. Once you crank out one of these vegan delights, you will feel like the no-bake dessert champ. Pull the tart from the freezer, and let it thaw for 30 minutes before serving. If you prefer a creamier texture over that of ice cream cake, you can store the tart in the refrigerator after the initial 6 to 8 hours in the freezer, which is the time necessary for the tart to set.

For the filling

2 cups raw
   unsalted cashews
1 cup blueberries, plus
   more for decoration
¾ cup water
¾ cup maple syrup
½ cup coconut
   oil, melted
Zest and juice
   of 1 lemon
1 teaspoon
   vanilla extract
Pinch salt

To make the filling

1. In a mixing bowl, cover the cashews with water, and let them sit overnight. Drain and rinse the cashews.

2. In a blender, combine the cashews, blueberries, water, maple syrup, coconut oil, lemon zest and juice, vanilla, and salt. Blend until the mixture is ultra-smooth and creamy.

To make the crust

3. Put the walnuts, coconut, dates, almond butter, and salt in a food processor. Pulse the ingredients together until the texture resembles very coarse wet sand.

4. Swipe the inside of an 8-inch springform pan with coconut oil. Press the walnut crumb mixture into an even layer in the bottom of the pan.

continued >>

For the crust

1 cup walnuts

1 cup flaked coconut

½ cup pitted dates

2 tablespoons
   almond butter

Pinch salt

Coconut oil, for
   greasing the pan

5. Pour the filling over the crust in the springform pan. Pick up and drop the pan a couple of times to help knock out any trapped air bubbles and to even out the filling layer. Dot the top of the tart with additional blueberries, then freeze for 6 to 8 hours.

Cooking 101: Soaking the cashews helps soften them and makes for a creamier result after blending. Soaking raw nuts before use also aids digestibility by removing compounds called phytates. Do not soak longer than 10 hours or so; after that time the nuts will turn bitter and the water slimy.

Per Serving (1 slice) Calories: 612; Total Fat: 45g; Saturated Fat: 20g; Sodium: 70mg; Carbohydrates: 51g; Fiber: 5g; Sugars: 34g; Protein: 8g

DIVIDE & CONQUER:
After the cashews have soaked, partner 1 can blend the filling while partner 2 makes the crust.

Lemon Ricotta Pancakes
with Blueberry Butter Syrup, page 58

30 Minutes

Cranberry-Coconut Granola

GLUTEN-FREE OPTION, VEGETARIAN, VEGAN OPTION

Makes 4 cups / Prep time: 5 minutes / Cook time: 25 minutes, plus 45 minutes to 1 hour to cool

Having a delicious granola recipe under your belt is a great way to treat yourselves to delightful, ready-to-go breakfasts. Or you can make a batch and leave it in a jar on the counter, so you can grab a handful to snack on at any time of day. The coconut tends to cook pretty quickly—keep an eye out for the perfectly toasty flakes while baking, so you don't end up with Cranberry–Burnt Coconut Granola.

2 cups rolled oats
   (or gluten-free
   rolled oats)
½ cup pumpkin seeds
½ cup chopped pecans
½ teaspoon salt
½ teaspoon ground
   cinnamon
½ teaspoon
   ground ginger
¼ cup melted
   salted butter (or
   coconut oil)
¼ cup honey (or
   maple syrup)
⅓ cup dried cranberries
⅓ cup unsweetened
   flaked coconut

1. Preheat the oven to 350°F. Line a baking sheet with parchment paper.

2. In a large mixing bowl, stir together the oats, pumpkin seeds, pecans, salt, cinnamon, and ginger.

3. Add the butter, honey, and dried cranberries. Stir until the oat mixture is well coated.

4. Dump the wet granola onto the prepared baking sheet, and use the back of a rubber spatula to spread it out in an even layer.

5. Transfer the baking sheet to the oven, and bake for 15 minutes. Then, pull out the baking sheet and stir in the coconut flakes, being careful not to break up the clumps too much so the granola will remain nice and chunky. Pat the granola back down a bit using the spatula, and put the baking sheet back in the oven for 10 minutes, or until golden. Remove from the oven. Let the granola cool for 45 minutes to 1 hour.

6. Enjoy the granola with milk, as a topper on yogurt, or straight from the pan. Store in an airtight container for up to 2 weeks or in a freezer-safe bag in the freezer for up to 3 months.

....

Mix it up: There are so many different ingredients you can add to make this granola your own. Try buckwheat groats, different nuts, seeds, dried mango, or mulberries. For some spice, add a bit of chili powder or allspice.

....

Per Serving (½ cup) Calories: 361; Total Fat: 27g; Saturated Fat: 15g; Sodium: 173mg; Carbohydrates: 29g; Fiber: 4g; Sugars: 13g; Protein: 6g

DIVIDE & CONQUER:
Partner 1 can preheat the oven, melt the butter or coconut oil, and measure out the honey while partner 2 combines the dry ingredients and mixes everything together.

Cinnamon Granola Berry Parfaits

GLUTEN-FREE OPTION, VEGETARIAN, VEGAN OPTION

Makes 4 parfaits / Prep time: 10 minutes / Cook time: 20 minutes

Parfaits are a longtime favorite of mine—I especially love being able to see the different layers and the potential of all the perfect bites lined up and ready for eating. Having a jarred snack or breakfast on hand makes life for us as a couple just a touch easier, and we like knowing that we don't have to grab a packaged bar on the way out the door but can instead grab something homemade for a quick bite. I recommend making your parfaits in a mason jar (I use Ball, Weck, and Kerr brands).

1 cup rolled oats
    (or gluten-free
    rolled oats)
¼ cup chopped pecans
¼ cup pumpkin seeds
¼ cup maple syrup
¼ cup melted
    salted butter (or
    coconut oil)
½ teaspoon cinnamon
¼ teaspoon salt
½ cup berry jam, divided
32 ounces yogurt,
    any variety or
    flavor (or vegan
    yogurt), divided
¼ cup honey (or maple
    syrup), divided

1. Preheat the oven to 350°F. Line a baking sheet with parchment paper.

2. In a medium mixing bowl, combine the oats, pecans, pumpkin seeds, maple syrup, butter, cinnamon, and salt.

3. Dump the wet granola onto the prepared baking sheet, and use the back of a rubber spatula to spread it out in an even layer.

4. Transfer the baking sheet to the oven, and bake for 15 minutes. Then, remove from the oven, and stir. Return to the oven for 5 minutes at a time until golden and crunchy. Remove from the oven. Transfer the granola from the hot baking sheet to a fresh baking sheet, and spread the granola out. (This helps stop the cooking and helps the granola cool faster.) Allow the granola to cool for 5 to 10 minutes before handling.

5. Set out four jars or serving cups, and assemble the parfaits starting with a spoonful of jam at the bottom of each jar, followed by about ¼ cup of yogurt, a scant tablespoon of honey, and a handful of granola. Repeat the layering process 3 more times, ending with granola on top.

Swap it out: Sick of yogurt? Try swapping in chia pudding.

Per Serving (1 parfait) Calories: 725; Total Fat: 28g; Saturated Fat: 15g; Sodium: 274mg; Carbohydrates: 105g; Fiber: 3g; Sugars: 86g; Protein: 22g

DIVIDE & CONQUER:

Partner 1 can preheat the oven, prep the baking sheet, and get the parfait cups ready while partner 2 measures out the ingredients. Together, combine the ingredients for the granola, and bake it. When layering the parfaits, partner 1 can put in the jam layer while partner 2 can add the yogurt and honey layers.

Lemon Ricotta Pancakes with Blueberry Butter Syrup

COMFORT FOOD, NUT-FREE, VEGETARIAN

Makes 6 pancakes / **Prep time:** 10 minutes / **Cook time:** 15 minutes

My love and I make these pancakes when we feel like having a date but don't want to go out to a fancy brunch. Just plain ol' pancakes are delicious, so adding a few bells and whistles like the ricotta and lemon elevates an already luxe breakfast and makes it all the more special. If you aren't a fan of blueberries, raspberries and strawberries are also perfect for this brunchy delight.

For the pancakes

1 cup all-purpose flour
2 tablespoons sugar
¼ teaspoon
    baking powder
¼ teaspoon salt
1 large egg
½ cup ricotta cheese
1¼ cups milk
Zest and juice
    of 1 lemon
½ teaspoon
    vanilla extract
Butter, for greasing
    the pan

For the syrup

2 tablespoons
    salted butter
⅓ cup fresh or frozen
    blueberries
¼ cup maple syrup
Pinch salt

To make the pancakes

1. In a large mixing bowl, thoroughly whisk together the flour, sugar, baking powder, and salt.

2. In another large mixing bowl, whisk the egg, then add the ricotta, milk, lemon zest, lemon juice, and vanilla. Whisk together until well combined.

3. Add the wet ingredients to the dry ingredients. Using a rubber spatula, gently combine. Do not overmix; some lumps are okay.

4. In a large skillet, melt a small pat of butter over medium heat, and swirl it around so it just coats the bottom. Scoop about ⅓ cup of batter into the hot skillet for each pancake, being careful not to overcrowd the skillet. Allow the pancakes to cook for about 3 minutes. When bubbles form, flip the pancakes, and cook for about 2 minutes, or until golden on the other side. Transfer the cooked pancakes to plates, and repeat with the remaining batter.

To make the syrup

5. In a small saucepan, melt the butter over medium heat for 3 to 4 minutes, or until it just starts to brown. Add the blueberries, and cook for about 2 minutes. Finish by adding the maple syrup and salt. Remove from the heat. Pour the syrup over the plated pancakes and serve.

Cooking 101: Resist the urge to overmix your batter in step 3. Overmixing will create tough pancakes instead of light and fluffy ones. Also, let your batter rest for a few minutes before pouring it into the hot skillet.

Per Serving (1 pancake) Calories: 237; Total Fat: 9g; Saturated Fat: 5g; Sodium: 213mg; Carbohydrates: 33g; Fiber: 1g; Sugars: 16g; Protein: 7g

DIVIDE & CONQUER: *Partner 1 can work on the pancake mix while partner 2 makes the blueberry syrup. Both partners should take a swing at flipping the flapjacks to see who will be the official pancake flipper for breakfasts to come.*

Savory Buckwheat Waffles with Soft Scrambled Eggs

COMFORT FOOD, GLUTEN-FREE, NUT-FREE, VEGETARIAN

Serves 2 / Prep time: 15 minutes / Cook time: 15 minutes

When we feel the urge for savory breakfasts, we often go with this dish. It is almost like an egg and cheese breakfast sandwich, but with a twist. Buckwheat is a hearty whole grain with a nutty and earthy flavor. Paired with kale and salty Parmesan cheese, you have a waffle fit for breakfast, lunch, or even dinner (just add fried chicken).

For the waffles

½ cup buckwheat flour
1 teaspoon sugar
¼ teaspoon
    baking powder
¼ teaspoon salt
1 large egg
¾ cup milk
2 kale leaves, stemmed
    and sliced into
    thin ribbons
¼ cup freshly grated
    Parmesan cheese
Butter, for greasing the
    waffle iron

For the eggs

3 large eggs
1 tablespoon
    salted butter
Pinch salt

To make the waffles

1. Preheat the waffle iron to high.

2. In a medium mixing bowl, thoroughly whisk together the flour, sugar, baking powder, and salt.

3. In a small mixing bowl, whisk together the egg and milk, then pour into the dry ingredients. Using a rubber spatula, gently combine until just incorporated.

4. Fold in the kale and Parmesan cheese.

5. Butter or oil the waffle iron. Scoop about ⅓ cup of batter into the waffle maker at a time. Let the waffle get to a deep golden brown before removing, about 5 minutes. Repeat with the remaining batter.

To make the eggs

6. In a small mixing bowl, vigorously beat the eggs with a fork for no less than 1 minute.

7. In a small skillet, melt the butter over low heat. When it has just melted, pour in the eggs and add the salt. There should be no sizzle.

8. Using a rubber spatula, fold the beaten eggs gently, only a few times a minute, for about 5 minutes, or until the eggs are just cooked, leaving them soft and bright yellow. Remove from the heat. Serve the eggs on top of or alongside the savory waffles.

Mix it up: Try poached or fried eggs instead of scrambled; the runny yolk is a great saucy addition. Or try a drizzle of honey and hot sauce over the waffles.

Per Serving Calories: 406; Total Fat: 22g; Saturated Fat: 11g; Sodium: 792mg; Carbohydrates: 29g; Fiber: 4g; Sugars: 7g; Protein: 23g

DIVIDE & CONQUER:
Partner 1 can make the waffles while partner 2 makes the soft scramble.

Grilled Cheese for Two

COMFORT FOOD, NUT-FREE, VEGETARIAN

Serves 2 / Prep time: 5 minutes / **Cook time:** 10 minutes

This concept of the grilled cheese for two is the actual pride and joy of our relationship. The idea came to us after several occasions in which one grilled cheese sandwich each left us hungry, but two grilled cheese sandwiches each was too many. We landed on the fact that three grilled cheeses total—one and a half each—has got to be the sweet spot. We would have opened a lunch shop if more brilliant ideas like this came to us, but alas, we have only perfected the Grilled Cheese for Two, and hey, we are thrilled with that.

3 tablespoons Dijon mustard

6 sourdough bread slices

12 Swiss or Cheddar cheese slices

6 tomato slices (optional)

6 tablespoons sauerkraut (optional)

2 tablespoons salted butter

3 tablespoons mayonnaise, divided

1. Spread a thin layer of mustard onto each slice of bread.

2. Stack the cheese, tomato (if using), and sauerkraut (if using) on top of the mustard side of 3 pieces of bread. Top each sandwich with another piece of bread, mustard-side down.

3. Melt the butter in a large skillet over medium-low heat. Spread an even layer of mayonnaise on top of the sandwiches, reserving enough for the other side once they are in the skillet. When the butter is hot, place the sandwiches in the skillet, mayonnaise-side down. Spread the rest of the mayonnaise on top of each sandwich.

4. Let the bread brown, slow and low over medium-low heat, adjusting to a lower heat if needed. Once the first side is perfectly golden, after 4 to 5 minutes, flip the sandwiches, then cover the skillet to help the cheese melt. After another 4 to 5 minutes, check to see if the bread has perfectly browned on that side. Remove from the heat.

5. Let the grilled cheeses cool slightly, slice each sandwich in half, and serve 3 halves each.

....

Swap it out: Using Gruyère, white Cheddar, or Monterey Jack cheeses instead of traditional Cheddar or Swiss cheese is a fun way to change up this favorite. Add thin slices of apple for a fun addition.

....

Per Serving Calories: 1,055; Total Fat: 64g; Saturated Fat: 29g; Sodium: 1,634mg; Carbohydrates: 66g; Fiber: 3g; Sugars: 6g; Protein: 42g

DIVIDE & CONQUER:
Partner 1 can gather the ingredients while partner 2 warms the skillet with the butter. Build the sandwiches together. Then, partner 1 can keep an eye on the sandwiches while partner 2 quickly cleans up.

Mediterranean Melt Sandwiches

COMFORT FOOD, VEGETARIAN

Makes 2 sandwiches / Prep time: 5 minutes / Cook time: 10 minutes

When a plain old grilled cheese isn't doing it for you, give this Mediterranean-inspired sammy a try. Use fresh mozzarella or buffalo mozzarella instead of sliced or shredded mozzarella. The fresh version tastes unmistakably better and melts really well, too. With herbaceous and salty pesto and tangy sun-dried tomatoes, it makes for a combination that can't be beat.

2 tablespoons mayon-
naise, divided

1 tablespoon prepared
basil pesto

4 sourdough or
multi-grain
bread slices

4 buffalo mozzarella
cheese slices

⅓ cup sun-dried toma-
toes, drained

½ cup loosely packed
fresh spinach

Salt

2 tablespoons
salted butter

1. In a small mixing bowl, combine 1 tablespoon of mayonnaise with the pesto. Mix well. Spread a thick layer on one side of each piece of the bread.

2. On 2 pieces of bread, start building the sandwiches by placing the mozzarella on top of the pesto mayonnaise, then layering on the sun-dried tomatoes, spinach, and a sprinkle of salt. Top with the remaining slices of bread, pesto mayonnaise–side down.

3. In a large skillet, melt the butter over medium heat. Spread a thin layer of the remaining 1 tablespoon of mayonnaise on top of the sandwiches, reserving enough for the other sides once they are in the skillet.

4. When the butter is hot, place the sandwiches in the skillet, mayonnaise-side down. Spread the remaining mayonnaise on top of each sandwich.

5. Let the bread brown for 4 to 5 minutes, or until golden, then flip the sandwiches and cover the skillet to help the cheese melt. Cook for 4 to 5 minutes. Adjust the heat as you go to ensure the cheese has melted and the outsides get golden and crisp. Remove from the heat.

Ingredient tip: You can make your own pesto at home in lieu of purchasing it. Enjoy it on pastas and in eggs as well. To make your own, put 2 cups fresh basil, 2 minced garlic cloves, ½ cup pine nuts, the juice of 1 lemon, ½ cup olive oil, ⅓ cup Parmesan, and ¼ teaspoon salt in a food processor. Pulse to desired consistency. Or you can change it up and try Arugula-Pecan Pesto (page 179).

Per Serving (1 sandwich) Calories: 660; Total Fat: 43g; Saturated Fat: 17g; Sodium: 911mg; Carbohydrates: 49g; Fiber: 3g; Sugars: 4g; Protein: 20g

> **DIVIDE & CONQUER:**
> *Partner 1 can gather the ingredients while partner 2 warms the skillet with the butter. Build the sandwiches together. Then, partner 1 can keep an eye on the sandwiches while partner 2 quickly cleans up.*

Caesar Salad with Fried Kale and Pine Nuts

DATE NIGHT, GLUTEN-FREE

Serves 2 / **Prep time:** 20 minutes / **Cook time:** 5 minutes

Caesar salad is great as a light entrée or a starter. Anchovies might freak out a few souls, but I urge you to keep an open mind; it's a staple for a classic Caesar salad. I add crispy kale and toasted pine nuts in lieu of croutons, but feel free to serve this with a fat piece of focaccia or a fresh roll.

For the salad

3 hearts of
    romaine, chopped
¼ cup pine nuts
1 cup avocado oil
3 kale leaves, stemmed
    and cut into
    thin ribbons

For the dressing

3 oil-packed
    anchovy fillets
1 large garlic clove
¼ teaspoon salt, plus
    more as needed
1 large egg yolk
1 teaspoon
    Dijon mustard
Zest and juice of
    ½ lemon
¼ cup avocado oil
2 tablespoon olive oil
¼ cup freshly grated
    Parmesan cheese
Freshly ground
    black pepper

To make the salad

1. Line a platter or a baking sheet with paper towels.

2. Put the romaine in a large serving bowl. Keep chilled in the refrigerator until needed.

3. In a dry medium skillet (which means no added fat), toast the pine nuts over medium-high heat for 2 to 3 minutes, or until just browned. This happens quickly, so watch the pine nuts closely, and give them a toss and a stir periodically as they toast. Remove from the heat. Transfer to a small mixing bowl.

4. In the same skillet, heat the avocado oil over medium heat until hot. Stick a toothpick in the oil and if bubbles collect around the tip, you are ready to fry. Working in three batches, fry the kale, stirring as it crisps and pops, for about 30 seconds. Using a slotted spoon or tongs, lift the kale out of the oil, and lay in a single layer on top of the paper towels. Sprinkle with salt.

To make the dressing

5. Mound the anchovies, garlic, and salt on a cutting board. Using the side of a chef's knife, chop and mash the ingredients until a paste has formed, scraping back and forth with the flat side of your knife as you go.

6. In a medium mixing bowl, whisk together the egg yolk, mustard, and lemon zest and juice.

7. In a measuring cup with a pour spout, or in a squeeze bottle, mix the avocado oil and olive oil together. While whisking vigorously, slowly drizzle the oils into the egg yolk mixture. (I do mean slowly—only a few drops at time.) Gradually the mixture will become glossy and thick, like mayonnaise. If you prefer a pourable creamy dressing, add water by the teaspoon to thin it out to your desired consistency.

8. Whisk in the anchovy paste and Parmesan cheese. Taste, and season with more salt and pepper, if needed.

9. Assemble the salad by tossing the romaine with plenty of dressing and topping with the fried kale and toasted pine nuts. Divide between two plates.

DIVIDE & CONQUER: *Partner 1 can start working on the salad by lining a platter with paper towels, prepping the romaine, and frying the kale while partner 2 tries their hand at making the dressing. Partner 1 may need to step in and drizzle the oil into the dressing—it needs to be painfully slow—as partner 2 whisks.*

Cooking 101: Emulsification is the act of combining two ingredients that ordinarily do not mix easily. The egg yolk, mustard, and process of slowly drizzling the olive oil into the dressing while whisking all aid emulsification to create a coherent and creamy dressing.

Per Serving Calories: 894; Total Fat: 87g; Saturated Fat: 12g; Sodium: 863mg; Carbohydrates: 11g; Fiber: 4g; Sugars: 3g; Protein: 13g

Panzanella Salad with Radicchio, Asiago, and Olives

NUT-FREE, VEGETARIAN

Serves 2 / Prep time: 10 minutes / Cook time: 20 minutes

Panzanella is a classic "bread salad" that is typically made with tomatoes and onions. You can liven it up with roasted red peppers, marinated artichokes, mozzarella cheese balls, herbs, or salami. With this version, I have flipped tradition on its head by using meaty olives, sweetly sharp Asiago cheese, seasoned and toasty focaccia, and bright and slightly bitter radicchio. Give both versions a try, and just try to pick a favorite.

For the salad

2 cups cubed
    focaccia (or torn
    into bite-size pieces)
2 tablespoons olive oil
Salt
1 small head radicchio
1 small cucumber
¼ red onion
½ cup grape tomatoes
½ cup Castelvetrano
    olives, pitted
    and halved
½ cup arugula
1 wedge Asiago cheese
Freshly ground
    black pepper

To make the salad

1. Preheat the oven to 350°F.

2. Put the focaccia in a large mixing bowl. Drizzle with the olive oil, and season with salt. Spread out on a baking sheet, transfer to the oven, and toast for 8 to 10 minutes. Stir and flip the bread. Toast for another 8 to 10 minutes, or until the croutons are golden. Remove from the oven.

3. While the focaccia is in the oven, cut the radicchio into thick ribbons, and put in a large serving bowl. Peel, seed, and chop the cucumber; thinly slice the onion; and halve the grape tomatoes, adding all to the serving bowl along with the olives and arugula.

4. Using a vegetable peeler, shave the Asiago cheese over the serving bowl, using as much as desired. Season with pepper.

For the vinaigrette

2 tablespoons
    red-wine vinegar

2 teaspoons honey

1 teaspoon
    Dijon mustard

1 teaspoon
    minced garlic

¼ cup olive oil

½ teaspoon salt

Freshly ground
    black pepper

To make the vinaigrette

5. In a small mixing bowl, whisk together the vinegar, honey, mustard, and garlic. While streaming in the olive oil, continue to whisk. Add the salt and several turns of freshly ground black pepper. Drizzle the vinaigrette over the salad, toss, and serve.

Prep tip: If making this salad in advance, you can prep the ingredients, except for the bread, and dress the salad. Toast the bread and mix it in just before serving. Day-old bread is also okay for this recipe and will toast more quickly.

Per Serving Calories: 1,269; Total Fat: 91g; Saturated Fat: 31g; Sodium: 2,819mg; Carbohydrates: 75g; Fiber: 6g; Sugars: 12g; Protein: 44g

---

DIVIDE & CONQUER:

Partner 1 can make the focaccia croutons according to steps 1 and 2 while partner 2 mixes up the dressing. Work together to chop the vegetables and assemble the salad (steps 3 and 4).

Chili-Lime Shrimp Salad

GLUTEN-FREE, NUT-FREE

Serves 2 / **Prep time:** 5 minutes / **Cook time:** 5 minutes

For such a simple salad, this really packs a lot of flavor. The chili-lime vinaigrette is so satisfyingly lip-smacking, tangy, and sweet. You can omit the shrimp if it is not your thing—lump crab, salmon, or pulled chicken would also be delightful.

For the salad

2 hearts of romaine, chopped

1 cup cherry tomatoes, halved

1 avocado, pitted and sliced

½ bunch fresh cilantro, stemmed

16 shrimp, shelled

1 tablespoon salted butter

Pinch chili powder

Pinch salt

For the dressing

Juice of 1 lime

2 teaspoons honey

1 tablespoon olive oil

¼ teaspoon chili powder, plus more as needed

¼ teaspoon salt, plus more as needed

To make the salad

1. In a large serving bowl, combine the romaine, tomatoes, avocado, and cilantro.

2. Pat the shrimp dry with paper towels. In a large skillet, melt the butter over medium-high heat. Add the shrimp, and sprinkle with the chili powder and salt. Cook for 1 to 2 minutes, then flip and cook for 1 to 2 minutes, or until the shrimp become just opaque. Remove from the heat. Let cool slightly. Add the shrimp to the salad.

To make the dressing

3. In a small mixing bowl, whisk together the lime juice, honey, olive oil, chili powder, and salt. Drizzle the vinaigrette over the salad, and toss. Adjust the seasoning to taste by adding more chili powder or salt.

Ingredient tip: A bag of frozen wild-caught shrimp is fantastic to have on hand if there is room in your freezer. They take very little time to thaw, and a handful of shrimp added to a salad like this is an easy way to make an entrée in no time.

Per Serving Calories: 375; Total Fat: 27g; Saturated Fat: 7g; Sodium: 481mg; Carbohydrates: 22g; Fiber: 10g; Sugars: 10g; Protein: 14g

DIVIDE & CONQUER:
Partner 1 can assemble the salad ingredients and cook the shrimp while partner 2 mixes up the dressing.

Spinach and Feta Burgers with Tomato, Red Onion, and Homemade Ranch Dressing

NUT-FREE, VEGETARIAN

Makes 2 burgers / Prep time: 10 minutes, plus 10 minutes to chill /
Cook time: 10 minutes

A dear friend in college, Sarah, used to make these burgers for me, and at the time I thought, "These are the best things I have ever put in my face." When I met my partner, I made these for him a few years into the relationship, and he wondered why I had been withholding them from him because they were also, in fact, "the best things that he had ever put in his face." We love to prepare them at least once a week to have on hand for eggs in the morning, served just as a patty, and, of course, as burgers. If you two are trying to do Meatless Mondays, this will be a hit. You can easily make these patties smaller by dividing the mix into four portions instead of two, if you wish.

For the ranch dressing

¼ cup mayonnaise

1 tablespoon
sour cream

1 tablespoon
plain yogurt

Zest and juice
of 1 lemon

1 tablespoon chopped
fresh dill

1 tablespoon chopped
fresh parsley

5 fresh chives,
finely chopped

½ teaspoon minced
red onion

½ teaspoon sugar

To make the ranch dressing

1. In a small mixing bowl, whisk the mayonnaise in order to work out any lumps. Add the sour cream, yogurt, lemon zest and lemon juice, dill, parsley, chives, onion, sugar, garlic powder, onion powder, and salt. Drizzle in the water by the teaspoon if a thinner consistency is desired.

To make the burgers

2. Chop half of the onion into rings. Finely dice the other half.

3. Thaw the spinach, and wring out as much water as possible. Put the spinach in a medium mixing bowl and add the feta cheese.

¼ teaspoon
    garlic powder
¼ teaspoon
    onion powder
½ teaspoon salt
1 to 2 tablespoons water

For the burgers

1 small red
    onion, divided
1 (12-ounce) package
    frozen spinach
2 ounces feta cheese,
    crumbled
1 garlic clove, minced
1 large egg
½ cup panko
    bread crumbs
Pinch salt
½ cup avocado oil
2 burger buns
1 tomato, sliced

4. Add the diced onion, garlic, egg, bread crumbs, and salt. Mix together until well combined. Form 2 large patties or 4 small ones. Put the patties on a plate, and refrigerate for about 10 minutes.

5. In a large skillet, heat the avocado oil over medium heat. When the oil is hot, add the patties, and cook for 2 to 3 minutes, reducing the heat to low so the patties stay golden. Flip, and cook for 2 to 3 minutes, or until golden on each side. Remove from the heat.

6. Split open the buns, and pile on the patties, sliced red onion, tomato, and ranch dressing.

Kitchen hack: No need to be above a packet of ranch seasoning purchased from the store. For a major shortcut, pick one up and follow the package instructions to make the ranch dressing.

Per Serving (1 burger) Calories: 1,124; Total Fat: 92g; Saturated Fat: 18g; Sodium: 1,438mg; Carbohydrates: 58g; Fiber: 9g; Sugars: 9g; Protein: 21g

---

DIVIDE & CONQUER:
Partner 1 can make the ranch dressing while partner 2 mixes up the burger ingredients in steps 2 through 4. Assemble, garnish, and dress the burgers together.

Fondue for Two

DATE NIGHT, GLUTEN-FREE OPTION,
NUT-FREE, VEGETARIAN OPTION

Serves 2 / Prep time: 20 minutes / **Cook time:** 10 minutes

There is nothing more comforting, classic, and, I suppose, a bit old school than a great fondue. My mom makes this for us on New Year's Day, and it is always a delight to pick and choose what to dip into this unmistakably boozy Alpine cheese dish. As long as you partake in cheese eating, there is something here for everyone, from potatoes and radishes to hunks of bread and sausage. It is a celebration in a cauldron.

4 ounces firm Alpine cheese, such as Gruyère or Comté

4 ounces Gouda cheese

4 ounces Fontina cheese

1 tablespoon cornstarch

2/3 cup dry white wine

1 garlic clove, minced

1½ teaspoons freshly squeezed lemon juice

1½ teaspoons brandy

½ teaspoon Dijon mustard

Pinch freshly grated nutmeg

1. Grate the Alpine cheese, Gouda, and Fontina into a medium mixing bowl. Add the cornstarch, and toss to thoroughly coat.

2. In an oven-safe fondue pot or a heavy-bottomed small Dutch oven or skillet, bring the wine, garlic, and lemon juice to a simmer over low heat. Add the cheese in thirds, stirring to ensure that each third is melted and whisked smooth before adding the next. Finish by adding the brandy and mustard. Grate in a bit of whole nutmeg. Stir to incorporate. Remove from the heat.

3. Arrange bite-size dippers on a platter. Serve with skewers or forks. Dip into the cheese, and enjoy.

Cubed fresh bread (such as French, sourdough, or pumpernickel), roasted baby potatoes, grape tomatoes, lightly steamed broccoli or cauliflower florets, radishes, tart apple slices (such as Granny Smith), or sliced cooked sausage, for serving

Kitchen hack: A fondue pot is all good and great, but a heavy cast-iron pan or Dutch oven will also do the trick when making this dish for two, since they both retain heat to keep the cheese melty while you eat. If you multiply the recipe for a bigger crowd, you can use a slow cooker or a double boiler to keep the cheese melty.

Per Serving Calories: 748; Total Fat: 52g; Saturated Fat: 32g; Sodium: 1,143mg; Carbohydrates: 8g; Fiber: 0g; Sugars: 5g; Protein: 46g

DIVIDE & CONQUER:
Partner 1 can prepare the cheese dipping sauce while partner 2 assembles the dippers.

Almond and Parmesan Chicken with Maple-Dijon Dip

GLUTEN-FREE

Serves 2 / Prep time: 5 minutes / Cook time: 25 minutes

When I was little, my mom would make a version of this for us, and for some reason, I called it "Aunt Betty's Chicken," even though there is no such aunt to speak of. We'll chalk it up to a child's imagination (although we did have a cat named Betty). These days, we add this delicious almond-Parmesan crust to anything we can get our hands on: fish, zucchini, and eggplant being among our favorites. This has the crispiness of a fried breading, but with a toasted nut and Parmesan flavor. It's like grown-up chicken fingers with dip.

½ cup mayonnaise, plus 2 tablespoons, divided

Juice of ½ lemon

1 cup whole almonds

1 cup freshly shredded Parmesan cheese

¼ teaspoon salt

8 chicken tenders

Olive oil, for drizzling

¼ cup Dijon mustard

¼ cup maple syrup

1. Preheat the oven to 350°F. Line a baking sheet with parchment paper.

2. In a medium mixing bowl, whisk ½ cup of mayonnaise in order to work out any lumps. Whisk in the lemon juice.

3. Put the almonds in a food processor, and pulse until they are the size of bread crumbs (irregular-size crumbs are okay). Add the Parmesan and salt. Pulse once or twice more to mix together. Dump out onto a large plate.

4. Dip each piece of chicken first into the mayonnaise mixture, coating evenly and scraping off any excess, then into the almond mixture, slightly packing it on to ensure a thick and even coating. Lay each breaded chicken tender out on the prepared baking sheet.

5. Drizzle oil over each piece of chicken, transfer the baking sheet to the oven, and bake for 25 minutes, or until golden brown. Remove from the oven.

6. In a small mixing bowl, whisk the remaining 2 tablespoons of mayonnaise to remove any lumps. Whisk in the mustard and maple syrup.

7. Serve the chicken with the sauce on the side for dipping.

Kitchen hack: I find that using pie dishes are best for making items that require dredging. They are the right size and have a lip so ingredients stay contained and do not fall off as they might from a plate.

Per Serving Calories: 1,604; Total Fat: 105g; Saturated Fat: 18g; Sodium: 2,189mg; Carbohydrates: 43g; Fiber: 9g; Sugars: 28g; Protein: 119g

DIVIDE & CONQUER:
Partner 1 can complete steps 1 through 3 while partner 2 mixes up the dipping sauce (step 6). Then, work together in assembly-line fashion to complete step 4: Partner 1 can coat the chicken in the mayonnaise, and partner 2 can dredge it in the almond mixture and put it on the baking sheet.

Chicken Marsala with Mushrooms Two Ways

COMFORT FOOD, GLUTEN-FREE OPTION, NUT-FREE

Serves 2 / **Prep time:** 5 minutes / **Cook time:** 25 minutes

The tiny twist on classic chicken Marsala here is the use of the shiitake mushrooms instead of the usual cremini mushrooms. The crispy shiitakes in this recipe, which we admiringly call "shiitake bacon," add the perfect salty crunch. Even if you aren't a mushroom lover, give this crispy twist a try.

12 ounces shiitake mushrooms, thinly sliced, divided

1½ teaspoons olive oil

Salt

2 boneless, skinless chicken breasts

3 tablespoons all-purpose flour (or rice flour)

Freshly ground black pepper

2 tablespoons salted butter

2 tablespoons minced shallot

2 garlic cloves, minced

⅓ cup Marsala wine

½ cup chicken broth

½ cup heavy cream

¼ bunch fresh parsley, stemmed and chopped

1. Preheat the oven to 375°F. Line a baking sheet with parchment paper.

2. Put 6 ounces of mushrooms on the prepared baking sheet, and toss them in the olive oil and a pinch of salt. Spread the mushrooms out in a single layer with plenty of room between slices, transfer to the oven, and roast for 10 minutes. Check to see if the mushrooms are dark brown and crisp. Roast in 1-minute increments thereafter, if necessary, until the mushrooms are perfectly browned. Remove from the oven.

3. Put the chicken breasts in a large zip-top bag (no need to seal it now, but you will need to seal it later). Using the flat end of a meat tenderizer, a rolling pin, or the bottom of a skillet, pound the chicken breasts until they are about ¼ inch thick. (If the breasts are very thick, slice them in half laterally before pounding. To do this, position your knife blade parallel to the cutting board, then start cutting at the thick end and cut carefully through the breast so that there is a top piece and a bottom piece. With 4 pieces of chicken, you may need an extra zip-top bag to do the pounding and seasoning.)

4. Put the flour, ¼ teaspoon of salt, and several turns of freshly ground black pepper into the bag with the chicken. Seal the top of the bag, and give it a good shake so that the pounded chicken is evenly coated with the flour and seasoning.

5. In a large skillet, melt the butter over medium-high heat. Shake off the excess flour from the chicken, and put the chicken in the skillet. Cook for about 3 minutes per side, or until the chicken is golden brown on both sides. Remove from the heat. Transfer the chicken to a place to rest while you make the sauce.

6. Put the remaining 6 ounces of mushrooms, the shallot, and garlic in the same skillet. Sauté for 3 to 4 minutes, or until caramelized. Pour in the Marsala wine. Stir, scraping up any browned bits.

7. Add the broth and cream, a couple pinches of salt and some freshly ground black pepper. Simmer for about 10 minutes, or until the sauce is reduced by half. Remove from the heat.

8. Slip the chicken back into the skillet, and top with the parsley and crispy roasted shiitakes.

DIVIDE & CONQUER: *Partner 1 can handle steps 1 and 2, keeping a watchful eye on the mushrooms while preparing and measuring the butter, shallot, garlic, wine, broth, cream, and parsley. Partner 2 can take care of the chicken, following steps 3 through 5. Both partners can work together to complete the sauce.*

Swap it out: Marsala is a fortified wine that should be found easily in the wine section of the grocery store or in a wine shop. Not a fan or can't find it? Try sherry, a dry white wine, or a medium-bodied red wine, if you'd prefer.

Per Serving Calories: 628; Total Fat: 40g; Saturated Fat: 22g; Sodium: 968mg; Carbohydrates: 43g; Fiber: 4g; Sugars: 9g; Protein: 29g

Spaghetti Carbonara

COMFORT FOOD, NUT-FREE

Serves 2 / Prep time: 5 minutes / Cook time: 25 minutes

Pasta carbonara originated in Rome and is traditionally made with Pecorino Romano or Parmigiano-Reggiano cheese. Any grated hard cheese will do; you can try aged provolone, Asiago, or my personal favorite, Grana Padano cheese. More is more, so feel free to add as much cheese as you'd like. This pasta dish is also stellar with tons of freshly ground black pepper. Retire the spaghetti and meatballs for a moment, and get your carbonara on.

8 ounces dried spaghetti

2 bacon slices

⅓ cup heavy cream

1 large egg yolk

¼ cup freshly grated
    Parmesan cheese

¼ cup peas

Salt

Freshly ground
    black pepper

1. Fill a large stockpot two-thirds full of water. Bring the water to a boil. Add the spaghetti, and cook until al dente, following the directions on the box. Reserve ¼ cup of cooking water before draining.

2. While waiting for the water to boil and the spaghetti to cook, heat a large skillet over medium-high heat, and chop the bacon. Add the bacon to the skillet, and cook for about 10 minutes, or until crisp. Transfer to a plate.

3. Pour the cream into the skillet. Simmer for 3 to 4 minutes, or until slightly reduced.

4. Add the spaghetti and reserved pasta water and stir.

continued >>

5. Add the egg yolk, Parmesan, peas, and bacon. Toss until the ingredients are incorporated and the pasta is well coated. Add a couple pinches of salt and several turns of freshly ground black pepper.

Swap it out: Try pancetta or guanciale instead of bacon if you are interested in changing it up. You want some kind of cured pork with enough fat content to ensure that your carbonara is creamy and flavorful.

Per Serving Calories: 697; Total Fat: 26g; Saturated Fat: 13g; Sodium: 434mg; Carbohydrates: 88g; Fiber: 5g; Sugars: 6g; Protein: 26g

DIVIDE & CONQUER:
Partner 1 can attend to the pasta cooking in step 1 while partner 2 completes step 2. Partner 2 can then continue making the sauce while partner 1 grates the cheese and assists partner 2 by adding the pasta to the skillet when ready.

Cannellini Bean and Bacon Succotash with Arugula

GLUTEN-FREE, NUT-FREE

Serves 2 / Prep time: 5 minutes / Cook time: 25 minutes

The word succotash *has Native American roots—from the Narragansett word* msíckquatash, *which means "boiled corn kernels." I love the name and wanted to keep it for this twist on the classic corn and lima bean medley. In this version, I've replaced the lima beans with cannellini beans, which are smooth and creamy and totally underutilized. They are great in dips, soups, and, as in this case, side dishes. I love this dish served under a pork chop, pork tenderloin, roasted chicken, or with crispy fried chicken. Add as many vegetables as you would like—zucchini or shredded sweet potatoes would be delicious additions.*

4 bacon slices

¼ yellow onion

1 celery stalk

¼ cup corn kernels, fresh or frozen

1 (15-ounce) can cannellini beans, rinsed and drained

2 tablespoons red-wine vinegar

1½ teaspoons honey

3 fresh thyme sprigs, stemmed

Pinch allspice

Pinch ground cumin

Pinch ground coriander

Salt

1. Heat a large skillet over medium-high heat. Chop the bacon, add to the skillet, and cook for 8 to 10 minutes, or until crisp. Reduce the heat if the bacon is browning too quickly.

2. Dice the onion, and thinly slice the celery. Add to the skillet, and cook for about 5 minutes. Add the corn, and sauté for about 2 minutes, or until soft.

3. Add the beans, vinegar, honey, thyme, allspice, cumin, coriander, a couple pinches of salt, and several turns of freshly ground black pepper. Toss for about 5 minutes, or until the flavors are incorporated and beans have warmed through.

continued >>

Freshly ground
    black pepper
1 cup arugula
1 lemon
1 tablespoon olive oil
2 ounces feta cheese,
    crumbled

4. Top with the arugula, and squeeze fresh lemon juice on top. Drizzle with the olive oil, and sprinkle with more salt and freshly ground black pepper, if desired. Toss together, top with the feta, and serve.

Kitchen hack: Ever open a can of beans and not use them all? Line a baking sheet with parchment paper and spread out any leftover rinsed and drained beans so there is lots of room between the beans. Freeze until solid, then put the beans in a zip-top bag. (This way they will be individually frozen rather than in a clump.) Grab a handful as needed and add to eggs, sautés, etc.

Per Serving Calories: 470; Total Fat: 22g; Saturated Fat: 8g; Sodium: 880mg; Carbohydrates: 51g; Fiber: 16g; Sugars: 8g; Protein: 25g

---

DIVIDE & CONQUER:
Partner 1 can chop the bacon, onion, and celery while partner 2 stems the thyme and rinses the beans. Partner 2 can begin sautéing the bacon while partner 1 adds the subsequent ingredients.

Lamb on a Stick with Wilted Spinach

DATE NIGHT, DAIRY-FREE, GLUTEN-FREE, NUT-FREE

Serves 2 / Prep time: 5 minutes / Cook time: 25 minutes

Rack of lamb is one of those impressive and often intimidating dishes that only seasoned cooks tend to even attempt. But you can do it. You can also buy your lamb frenched, which means that the fat and the meat are trimmed away, leaving the rib bones exposed. (This isn't exactly necessary; it just makes for a fancier presentation.) The great thing about lamb is that it is one of the only meats that is widely appreciated by even professional chefs when cooked at a variety of temperatures (meaning pink lamb is good and lamb cooked to medium-well is also good). This is a great dish to have in your repertoire, because it is delicious and looks impressive, yet the technique that it requires is very manageable. This is a fun dish to make together. Poof, you're fancy.

1 frenched rack of lamb
with 7 or 8 bones,
patted dry

1 teaspoon dried
rosemary

1 teaspoon
minced garlic

2 teaspoons olive oil,
plus more as needed

½ teaspoon salt

Freshly ground
black pepper

¼ cup balsamic vinegar

1½ tablespoons honey

2 cups fresh spinach

1. Preheat the oven to 375°F.

2. Heat a large, oven-safe heavy-bottomed skillet, like a cast-iron skillet. (The skillet should be dry, without any added fat.)

3. While the skillet heats, in a small bowl, combine the rosemary, garlic, olive oil, salt, and pepper to make a rub. Massage the rub into the fatty side of the lamb.

4. Lay the lamb, rub-side down, in the skillet to brown.

5. Rotate the lamb in the skillet with tongs, for about 5 minutes, browning it on all sides.

continued >>

6. Put the skillet in the oven. After about 15 minutes, use a meat thermometer to check the temperature. Remove the skillet from the oven when the lamb registers 135°F. Pull the lamb from the skillet, transfer it to a plate, and let it rest for about 5 minutes while you make the sauce.

7. Put the same skillet back on the stovetop over medium heat, pour in the vinegar and honey, and whisk to combine and scrape up the residual browned bits, for about 5 minutes. Pour the sauce into a small bowl. Turn off the heat.

8. Throw the spinach into the skillet, and sprinkle it with a few drops of olive oil and a pinch of salt. Put a lid on the skillet, and let the residual steam wilt the spinach in 30 to 45 seconds. Give the spinach a quick stir, and plate.

9. Slice the lamb between the ribs so that there are 7 or 8 pieces of "lamb on a stick." Arrange on top of the spinach, and drizzle with the balsamic honey pan sauce.

DIVIDE & CONQUER:

Partner 1 can take care of steps 1 and 2 while partner 2 pats the lamb dry and completes steps 3 through 5. While partner 2 is working with the lamb, partner 1 can measure out the rest of the ingredients. Partner 1 can take over once the lamb is resting by making the balsamic pan sauce and wilting the spinach while partner 2 tidies up.

....

Prep tip: If the lamb has a rather thick layer of fat, score it by making a few shallow cuts; this will help the lamb crisp and brown more evenly.

....

Per Serving Calories: 587; Total Fat: 43g; Saturated Fat: 20g; Sodium: 1,229mg; Carbohydrates: 22g; Fiber: 1g; Sugars: 13g; Protein: 29g

Old Bay Butter Shrimp and Corn Polenta

GLUTEN-FREE, NUT-FREE

Serves 2 / **Prep time:** 10 minutes / **Cook time:** 20 minutes

*When my fellow chef pal, Joel, told me that we were making polenta, I imme-
diately imagined thick corn grits, which are delicious, but it was a warm day,
and it did not seem fitting. He proceeded to cut fresh corn kernels from the
cob directly into hot butter. Then he sautéed them for a few minutes before
blitzing them in the blender. I was floored with the simplicity and the silkiness
of this kind of corn polenta. My partner and I have used fresh and frozen corn,
and both are delicious. It is a dish we hold dear. Thanks, Joel!*

For the polenta

2 tablespoons
    salted butter
1 (10-ounce) bag
    frozen corn
½ cup milk
1 teaspoon honey
½ teaspoon salt
¼ teaspoon chili powder

For the shrimp

16 shrimp, peeled
    and deveined
    (tail-on okay)
1½ tablespoons
    salted butter
1 teaspoon Old Bay
    seasoning
Pinch salt
2 scallions, green and
    white parts, sliced
    (optional)

To make the polenta

1. In a large skillet, melt the butter over
   medium-high heat. Add the corn. Sauté for 1 to
   2 minutes, or until thawed. Add the milk, honey,
   salt, and chili powder, stirring to incorporate.
   Simmer for about 10 minutes. Remove from
   the heat.

2. Let the corn mixture cool slightly before putting it into a blender. Using a rubber spatula
   to scrape down the sides as needed, blend the
   corn until very smooth. Add the puréed corn
   back to the skillet, or transfer to your preferred
   serving dish.

continued »

To make the shrimp

3. Pat the shrimp dry with paper towels. In a large skillet, melt the butter over medium-high heat. Add the shrimp, then sprinkle in the Old Bay seasoning and salt. Cook for 1 to 2 minutes, then flip the shrimp and cook for another 1 to 2 minutes, or until they just become opaque. Remove from the heat. Let cool slightly. Top the polenta with the shrimp, being sure to include the excess Old Bay and butter remnants from the skillet. Top with the scallions (if using).

> **DIVIDE & CONQUER:**
> *Partner 1 can make the polenta while partner 2 collects the ingredients for the shrimp and cooks them, timing their cooking so they are done at about the same time as the polenta.*

Ingredient tip: There is no shame in using frozen corn. Winter is for eating preserved, jarred, canned, and frozen foods that have been "put up" during the peak growing season. Make fresh corn polenta in the late summer when corn is at its finest.

Per Serving Calories: 373; Total Fat: 24g; Saturated Fat: 14g; Sodium: 1,188mg; Carbohydrates: 26g; Fiber: 1g; Sugars: 10g; Protein: 15g

Pecan Butter Halibut and Roasted Broccoli

DATE NIGHT, GLUTEN-FREE

Serves 2 / Prep time: 5 minutes / Cook time: 20 minutes

Halibut is a thick, buttery white fish that appeals even to people who do not usually like fish. Typically, a simple pan sear in some butter with a sprinkle of salt followed by finishing in the oven is how I like to treat this high-ticket item. But then I discovered this style of nut crust, thanks to a lovely little restaurant I frequent, and I got hooked. No pun intended. The pecan butter melts into the fish while cooking, adding even more flavor and richness.

For the broccoli

1 head broccoli
1½ teaspoons olive oil
Pinch salt

For the halibut

½ cup pecans
2 tablespoons
   salted butter
¼ teaspoon salt
Pinch allspice
Pinch paprika
Pinch chili powder
2 (3- to 4-ounce)
   halibut fillets

To make the broccoli

1. Preheat the oven to 375°F.

2. Cut the broccoli into bite-size florets (the florets will roast more evenly if they are roughly the same size).

3. Put the broccoli florets on a baking sheet, and toss with the olive oil and salt. Spread them out in a single layer with plenty of room between them. Transfer to the oven, and roast for 10 minutes. Then stir, continuing to roast for 2-minute intervals until the desired color and crispness is achieved. Remove from the oven.

To make the halibut

4. Line a separate baking sheet with parchment paper.

5. Put the pecans, butter, salt, allspice, paprika, and chili powder in a food processor. Pulse until a textured purée is achieved, almost like an extremely chunky peanut butter.

continued >>

PECAN BUTTER HALIBUT AND ROASTED BROCCOLI *continued*

6. Put the halibut fillets on the prepared baking sheet. Pack the pecan butter, about ¼ inch thick, on top of each halibut fillet. Transfer to the oven, and bake for 12 minutes for medium-well. (The halibut and the broccoli can be in the oven at the same time; just put the broccoli on the bottom rack and the halibut on the top.)

DIVIDE & CONQUER: *Partner 1 can focus on making the broccoli side dish, and partner 2 can make the pecan butter and cook the halibut.*

Ingredient tip: Frozen fish is often cheaper. It is packed and frozen minutes after being caught. Frozen seafood is a great way to go when you don't want to break the bank.

Per Serving Calories: 524; Total Fat: 38g; Saturated Fat: 10g; Sodium: 552mg; Carbohydrates: 20g; Fiber: 12g; Sugars: 6g; Protein: 34g

Panfried Thai Curry Wild Salmon Cakes

DAIRY-FREE, GLUTEN-FREE, NUT-FREE

Makes 6 salmon cakes / **Prep time:** 10 minutes / **Cook time:** 10 minutes

Red Thai curry is made from dried red chiles, lemongrass, garlic, shallots, and fish paste. It has an unmistakable sweetness, a touch of heat, and lots of flavor. We keep a jar of both red and green Thai curry paste on hand for vegetable curries, chicken, coconut milk–based soups, and, of course, fish cakes. Any salmon will work for this recipe. We love wild sockeye salmon, but when we are feeling rich, we go for wild king salmon as a treat.

1 pound fresh wild skinless salmon fillets, pin bones removed

1 teaspoon chopped fresh basil

1 teaspoon chopped fresh mint

1 teaspoon chopped fresh cilantro

1 tablespoon red Thai curry paste (or for a milder version, try green curry)

1 tablespoon tamari

1 scallion, green and white parts, chopped

1 garlic clove, minced

2 tablespoons avocado oil

1. Line a baking sheet with parchment paper.

2. Chop the salmon into large chunks, and put them in a food processor. Add the basil, mint, cilantro, curry paste, tamari, scallion, and garlic. Pulse a few times until just broken down and mixed well. Do not overprocess. The mixture should have lots of texture and should not be puréed.

3. Using a rubber spatula, scrape the salmon cake mixture into a large mixing bowl. Form 6 equal patties, and put them on the prepared baking sheet.

4. In a large skillet, heat the oil over medium-high heat. When the oil is hot, lay the cakes in the skillet with plenty of room between them. (Cook in two batches, if necessary.) After 3 to 4 minutes, slide an offset spatula under one of the cakes to gently lift and see if the cake is browned. Once browned, flip and cook for about 2 minutes, or until browned on the other side. Remove from the heat.

continued »

Kitchen hack: How do you know when your oil is hot? Stick one end of a toothpick in the oil, and if bubbles collect around the tip, it's ready. Always lay the item you are placing in the hot oil away from you to avoid splatter.

Per Serving (1 cake) Calories: 124; Total Fat: 6g; Saturated Fat: 1g; Sodium: 168mg; Carbohydrates: 1g; Fiber: <1g; Sugars: <1g; Protein: 16g

DIVIDE & CONQUER:

If you need to remove the skin and bones of the salmon yourself, partner 1 can wrestle with the salmon while partner 2 offers love and support. Otherwise, both partners can prep the ingredients. Then partner 1 can handle the food processing in step 2 while partner 2 lines the baking sheet and gets the skillet ready. Together you can form, fry, and flip the patties.

Maple-Dijon Salmon with Green Beans and Caramelized Shallot

GLUTEN-FREE, NUT-FREE

Serves 2 / Prep time: 5 minutes / Cook time: 25 minutes

Salmon is a go-to fish for my guy and me. We love king salmon and sockeye salmon, and we always opt for wild-caught. Salmon can be paired with a great many sauces, and this maple-Dijon sauce is a nod to the classic favorite, honey mustard. It is easy to mix up and makes for a great topper for the fish. With some easy green beans on the side, this dish is a perfect weeknight dinner.

For the green beans

1 tablespoon
   salted butter
1½ teaspoons olive oil
2 shallots, thinly sliced
8 ounces green
   beans, trimmed
2 teaspoons tamari
1 teaspoon maple syrup

For the salmon

1 tablespoon
   Dijon mustard
1 tablespoon
   maple syrup
Pinch salt
2 (3- to 4-ounce)
   salmon fillets

To make the green beans

1. In a medium skillet, heat the butter and olive oil over medium heat. Add the shallots and stir. Cover with a fitted lid, and reduce the heat to medium-low. Cook for about 20 minutes, stirring only briefly once or twice, or until caramelized. (The butter not only adds flavor but also will help keep the olive oil from overheating and smoking.)

2. Meanwhile, fill a medium saucepan two-thirds full of water, and bring to a boil. Add the green beans. Cook for about 4 minutes, or until they are fork-tender. Remove the green beans from the water, and add to the shallots.

3. Pour in the tamari and maple syrup. Toss together, and cook for 2 to 3 minutes. Remove from the heat.

continued >>

To make the salmon

4. While the shallots are cooking on the stovetop, preheat the oven to 350°F, and line a baking sheet with parchment paper.

5. In a small mixing bowl, whisk together the mustard, maple syrup, and salt.

6. Put the salmon on the prepared baking sheet, and spoon or brush the sauce over each piece of salmon. Transfer to the oven, and bake for about 12 minutes for medium-well. Remove from the oven. Serve with the green beans on the side.

> **DIVIDE &
> CONQUER:**
> *Partner 1 can make
> the green beans while
> partner 2 makes the
> sauce and cooks
> the salmon.*

Prep tip: If getting salmon fresh from the seafood section, go ahead and ask the folks behind the counter to remove the pin bones and the skin. They are happy to slice exactly how much you want from a larger fillet. Use them as a resource to ask what is fresh for the day. (Also, I have never met a fishmonger who doesn't have a great recipe up their sleeve that's ready to be shared.)

Per Serving Calories: 281; Total Fat: 13g; Saturated Fat: 5g; Sodium: 602mg; Carbohydrates: 21g; Fiber: 4g; Sugars: 13g; Protein: 21g

Brown Butter Crispy Rice Treats

GLUTEN-FREE, NUT-FREE, VEGETARIAN

Makes 10 squares / Prep time: 5 minutes / **Cook time:** 5 minutes, plus 10 minutes to cool

....

Who doesn't love the all-time classic marshmallow square? In my experience, you want it thick and chewy but airy, sweet but not too sweet (so you can eat two), and with slightly more marshmallow than necessary—but not so goopy that it doesn't stay together. I have taken the liberty of adding the luxurious flavors of brown sugar and brown butter, for a caramelly, toasty, salty flavor that bumps a childhood fave up a notch.

3 tablespoons salted butter, plus more for the spatula

1 tablespoon brown sugar

1 (10-ounce) bag marshmallows

½ teaspoon vanilla extract

¼ teaspoon flake salt

6 cups crispy rice cereal

1. Line a 9-by-13-inch baking dish with parchment paper.

2. In a large saucepan or Dutch oven, melt the butter and sugar over medium heat. Once the butter has melted, continue cooking until small brown bits form, swirling the pan to ensure the butter only browns and doesn't burn.

3. Stir in the marshmallows immediately, and continue stirring until melted. Add the vanilla and salt.

4. Gently mix in the cereal until well coated by the melted marshmallow batter. Remove from the heat.

continued >>

5. Turn out the gooey marshmallow and cereal mixture into the prepared baking dish. Using the back of a buttered rubber spatula, press the marshmallow-and-cereal mixture into the dish in an even layer. (Using your hands to firmly pack the treats will cause them to be set up more densely. Packing gently with a spatula will ensure that the treats stick together while staying more airy and chewy.)

6. Let cool for about 10 minutes before slicing.

Ingredient tip: Flake salt, like Maldon, is considered less bitter, less caustic, and has even been described as less salty than other more granular salts. A delicate flake salt like this one is great as a finishing salt to sprinkle on top of meat and vegetables. It is also perfect for sweets like salted caramel or for sprinkling on top of chocolate chip cookies before baking.

Per Serving (1 square) Calories: 197; Total Fat: 4g; Saturated Fat: 2g; Sodium: 214mg; Carbohydrates: 39g; Fiber: 0g; Sugars: 23g; Protein: 1g

> **DIVIDE & CONQUER:**
> *Partner 1 can line the baking dish while partner 2 completes step 2. Partner 1 can pour in the ingredients in the order they are called for while partner 2 stirs. Partner 2 can turn the mixture out onto the baking dish while partner 1 smooths it over with the rubber spatula.*

Banana Crème Brûlée, page 123

5 Ingredients

Blue Cheese and Scallion Scones

NUT-FREE, VEGETARIAN

Makes 4 scones / Prep time: 15 minutes / Cook time: 15 minutes

My partner and I are huge fans of biscuits and scones. Sweet or savory, with jam, butter, clotted cream, skillet gravy, eggs—you name it, we have a biscuit in mind for it. We don't typically take the time to distinguish the differences between the two, scones versus biscuits; however, it is said that biscuits should be fluffy and flaky and scones should be a little soft but dense and have a good crumble to them. I use this pretty basic recipe for all kinds of scone-y and biscuit-y things and add flavors to my liking. My husband's all-time favorite is these Blue Cheese and Scallion Scones . . . or biscuits, whatever.

1 cup all-purpose flour, plus more for dusting

Salt

4 tablespoons (½ stick) cold salted butter

¼ cup buttermilk or heavy cream, plus 1 tablespoon, divided

2 tablespoons crumbled blue cheese

2 scallions, green and white parts, chopped

1. Preheat the oven to 375°F. Line a baking sheet with parchment paper.

2. In a medium mixing bowl, whisk together the flour and a pinch of salt. Using a box grater, grate the butter into the bowl.

3. Working quickly, toss the butter into the flour so it is coated and distributed evenly. Pour in ¼ cup of buttermilk. Using your clean hands or a fork, gently work the mixture until a dough just comes together. No need to overmix; the dough is supposed to look shaggy.

4. Add the blue cheese and scallions. Gently fold the dough over a couple of times until evenly distributed. The trick is to work your dough as little as possible to keep your biscuits and scones from becoming tough.

5. Dust the counter with a little flour, and dump out the dough. With very little handling, form a disk and slice, like a pie, into 4 wedge-shaped scones.

6. Put the scones on the prepared sheet, and brush the remaining 1 tablespoon of buttermilk over them. Transfer to the oven, and bake for 15 minutes, or until golden brown on the bottom. Remove from the oven.

Swap it out: Try out different flavor combinations, such as apple-Cheddar, cherry-chocolate, or pear-cinnamon.

Per Serving (1 scone) Calories: 227; Total Fat: 13g; Saturated Fat: 8g; Sodium: 162mg; Carbohydrates: 24g; Fiber: 1g; Sugars: 1g; Protein: 5g

DIVIDE & CONQUER:
Partner 1 can take care of step 1 while partner 2 gets the dry ingredients together. Partner 1 can then grate in the butter, and partner 2 can follow steps 3 and 4 to make the dough. Partner 1 can then flour a surface, then can take over for partner 2 to complete steps 5 and 6.

Sweet Potato Fries with Garlic-Basil Aïoli

COMFORT FOOD, DAIRY-FREE, GLUTEN-FREE, VEGETARIAN

Serves 2 / Prep time: 10 minutes / **Cook time:** 40 minutes

Let's admit it: Deep-frying French fries at home is daunting. There's oil spattering everywhere, not to mention the problem of disposing of all the used oil afterward. That's why I've been on the lookout for the best oven fries—and I think I've found them. These sweet potato fries are roasted and crispy thanks to the slender cuts, the high heat of the oven, and the dusting of cornstarch. If you aren't a sweet potato fan, you can swap in a Yukon gold potato very easily.

For the fries

3 sweet potatoes
3 teaspoons corn-
    starch, divided
½ teaspoon salt, divided
2 tablespoons olive
    oil, divided

For the aïoli

¼ cup mayonnaise
1½ teaspoons
    dried basil
1 teaspoon
    minced garlic
Pinch salt
Freshly ground
    black pepper

To make the fries

1. Preheat the oven to 425°F.

2. Peel the sweet potatoes, cut into ¼-inch-thick slabs, then into ¼-inch-thick sticks. Try to keep the size as uniform as possible. If you have a wide range of sizes, the thin fries will burn, and the thicker fries will be undercooked.

3. Divide the fries between two baking sheets. Sprinkle each batch with 1½ teaspoons of cornstarch and ¼ teaspoon of salt. Gently massage the cornstarch and salt into the fries, making sure the cornstarch gets rubbed in and the salt is evenly distributed. On each baking sheet, arrange the fries in a single layer with lots of room between them so they will crisp and not steam.

4. Drizzle each batch of fries with 1 tablespoon of olive oil. Transfer the baking sheets to the oven, and roast for 20 minutes.

5. Pull the fries from the oven, and flip them. When you put them back in the oven, switch the position of the baking sheets (move the one that was on the top rack to the bottom rack and vice versa). Roast the fries for 15 to 20 minutes, or until they have a slightly matte appearance and are a bit puffed and crispy. Remove from the oven.

To make the aïoli

6. Whisk together the mayonnaise, basil, and garlic. Season with the salt and some freshly ground black pepper. Serve alongside the fries for dipping.

DIVIDE &
CONQUER:
Both partners can peel and slice the sweet potatoes. One partner can peel while the other slices and vice versa. This is a good opportunity to practice valuable knife skills. Then, partner 1 can finish preparing the fries (steps 3, 4, and 5) while partner 2 whips up the aïoli.

Cooking 101: Okay, you caught me, this is not a real aïoli, which is essentially a creamy condiment, like mayonnaise, but made with garlic and olive oil, and typically made by hand. Whereas mayonnaise is traditionally made with egg yolks and canola oil. This faux aïoli will work just fine. Mayonnaise brands like Duke's and Primal Kitchen mayonnaise are my favorites when I am using some for dipping.

Per Serving Calories: 545; Total Fat: 39g; Saturated Fat: 5g; Sodium: 796mg; Carbohydrates: 52g; Fiber: 6g; Sugars: 8g; Protein: 3g

Harissa and Honey-Roasted Carrots

DATE NIGHT, GLUTEN-FREE, NUT-FREE, VEGETARIAN

Serves 2 to 4 / Prep time: 10 minutes, plus overnight to chill / Cook time: 45 minutes

We tend to eat this dish as a main course since we eat so much of it in one sitting; otherwise, it is a wonderful and hearty side dish. You can dress this up for a fancier meal by using rainbow carrots and garnishing it with pumpkin or pomegranate seeds. I serve this dish with a traditional Middle Eastern strained yogurt spread known as labneh—it's a cinch to make.

For the labneh

1 cup full-fat
   plain yogurt
Olive oil, for drizzling
Salt
Zest and juice of 1 lime

For the carrots

10 to 12 rainbow slender
   medium carrots,
   with stem
¼ cup harissa paste
2 tablespoons honey
Salt

To make the labneh

1. At least 8 hours before you plan to make this dish, or even the night before, fit a mesh strainer into a mixing bowl so that there is room beneath the strainer for liquids to drain off. Line the mesh strainer with cheesecloth or a clean thin (we're talking almost see-through) dish towel. Using a rubber spatula, scrape all of the yogurt into the lined mesh strainer, then gently cover by folding over the sides of the cheesecloth or towel. Refrigerate for about 8 hours or overnight.

2. Transfer the yogurt (it will be much creamier) from the cloth to a clean medium mixing bowl. Add a drizzle of olive oil, a few pinches of salt, and the lime zest and juice. Stir together and return to the refrigerator until ready for use.

To make the carrots

3. Preheat the oven to 375°F.

4. Clean and dry the carrots. Trim the stems so they are no longer than ½ inch. Cut the carrots in half lengthwise, or quarters if more than ½ inch thick.

5. Put the carrots on a baking sheet. Coat the carrots with the harissa paste, honey, and a few pinches of salt. Spread the carrots out into an even layer. Transfer to the oven, and roast for 25 minutes.

6. Stir the carrots, and rotate the baking sheet, then roast for 20 minutes or so, or until they are caramelized and brown. Some parts may even look slightly charred (that's good). Remove from the oven.

7. Pile the carrots on a serving dish, and dollop with lots of labneh, finishing with a final drizzle of olive oil.

DIVIDE & CONQUER:
Partner 1 can assemble the lined strainer over a bowl while partner 2 scrapes in the yogurt. The next day, partner 1 can season the labneh while partner 2 prepares and cooks the carrots.

Kitchen hack: Roasting your vegetables on an unlined baking sheet helps them brown better. Parchment paper—lined baking and roasting sure makes for an easy cleanup, but when you want that roasted and caramelized flavor on your vegetables, go paperless.

Per Serving Calories: 293; Total Fat: 5g; Saturated Fat: 3g; Sodium: 368mg; Carbohydrates: 55g; Fiber: 10g; Sugars: 39g; Protein: 8g

Arugula Salad with Roasted Grapes and Walnut Dressing

DAIRY-FREE, GLUTEN-FREE, VEGETARIAN

Serves 2 / Prep time: 5 minutes / Cook time: 45 minutes

I don't remember when I started to roast grapes, but once I did, I never looked back. I love the ultra-sweet addition of the roasted, caramelized fruit in a bitter green salad. The walnut dressing is salty and earthy, creating a nice contrast. The dressing can be heavy on delicate greens like arugula, so be sure to dress just before serving to keep the salad looking fresh and light. If you eat dairy, add a little blue cheese or some Gorgonzola crumbles, if you have them.

½ cup red grapes
¼ cup olive oil, plus more for drizzling
Salt
2 cups arugula
½ cup walnuts, divided
1½ teaspoons honey
1½ tablespoons tamari

1. Preheat the oven to 350°F. Line a baking sheet with parchment paper.

2. Put the grapes on the prepared baking sheet. Drizzle a little bit of olive oil over them, add a sprinkle of salt, and gently toss to coat. Transfer to the oven, and roast for 45 minutes, or until they start to release juices. Remove from the oven. Let cool.

3. Arrange the arugula in a serving bowl. Add ¼ cup of walnuts and the grapes.

4. Put the remaining ¼ cup of walnuts, the honey, and the tamari in a blender. Blend, streaming in the olive oil and water by the spoonful until the dressing is thick, creamy, and smooth. Spoon the dressing over the salad, and toss, saving any extra dressing in a jar for later use. The refrigerated dressing will keep for up to 7 days.

Ingredient tip: While roasting, the grapes will plump at first, then the juices will slowly start to seep out, which is when you should remove them from the oven. They will then shrink down a bit as they cool. Any extra roasted grapes can be stored in a sealed container in the refrigerator for the next 4 to 5 days.

Per Serving Calories: 218; Total Fat: 17g; Saturated Fat: 2g; Sodium: 761mg; Carbohydrates: 16g; Fiber: 2g; Sugars: 11g; Protein: 6g

DIVIDE & CONQUER:

Partner 1 can roast the grapes and prep the arugula and walnuts by combining them in a serving bowl. Partner 2 can make the dressing.

Spinach and Feta Cheese Pastries

NUT-FREE, VEGETARIAN

Makes 2 pastries / Prep time: 10 minutes / Cook time: 45 minutes

Spanakopita is the traditional name for Greek spinach-and-cheese pie. Flaky layers of phyllo dough are typically used, but puff pastry allows you to avoid dealing with all of those easily torn, labor-intensive layers of phyllo pastry. Think of this spinach-and-feta hand pie as a shortcut to the more labor-intensive classic spanakopita.

1 large egg

1 sheet frozen puff pastry, thawed

1 tablespoon Dijon mustard

1 (10-ounce) package frozen spinach, thawed

Salt

4 ounces feta cheese, crumbled, divided

1. Preheat the oven to 375°F. Line a baking sheet with parchment paper.

2. In a small mixing bowl, whisk the egg.

3. Using a rolling pin, lightly roll out the puff pastry, so it is in a rough square shape (it doesn't have to be perfect) of an even thickness and the creases have been smoothed out. Cut the dough into fourths, slicing in half once lengthwise and once crosswise.

4. Brush the mustard onto the inside of 2 pastry pieces. Put 2 pieces of pastry on the prepared baking sheet.

5. Wring out the spinach very well, and divide it into 2 portions. Pile each portion into the center of the 2 pastry pieces on the baking sheet, leaving a ¼-inch border of exposed dough around the edges. Sprinkle the spinach with a little salt, then top with 2 ounces of feta cheese.

6. Brush the egg along the exposed edges of the 2 pastry squares on the baking sheet. Top each piece of filled pastry with one of the remaining pastry squares. Using the bottom side of the tines on a fork, press down around the edges of pastry on all sides to seal.

7. Stab the fork into the top of each pastry a few times so steam can escape during baking. Brush the remaining egg all over the top of both pastries.

8. Transfer the baking sheet to the oven, and bake for 40 to 45 minutes, or until puffed and golden brown. Remove from the oven.

Ingredient tip: Fresh spinach is not as user friendly in this recipe as frozen spinach because it adds extra steps to the process. But if you would like to use fresh spinach, steam 10 ounces, let cool, wring the water out, and chop before filling your pastry.

Per Serving (1 pastry) Calories: 908; Total Fat: 62g; Saturated Fat: 16g; Sodium: 1,231mg; Carbohydrates: 64g; Fiber: 5g; Sugars: 4g; Protein: 24g

DIVIDE & CONQUER:
Partner 1 can complete steps 1 and 2 while partner 2 presses on with steps 3 and 4. Together, partners 1 and 2 can fill the spinach-and-cheese pies. Then, partner 1 can brush the egg around the border while partner 2 follows behind with a fork to do the sealing and piercing of the top crust. Partner 1 can add the final brushes of egg on top before baking.

Tomato and Cheddar Savory Tart

NUT-FREE, VEGETARIAN

Serves 4 / **Prep time:** 20 minutes / **Cook time:** 50 minutes to 1 hour

I always have a savory tart recipe up my sleeve. A savory tart is simple, delicious, and hard to screw up. Whether you top it with a simple light salad, enjoy the reheated leftovers the next day, or bring it to a potluck or picnic to be served room temperature, the humble savory tart has you covered. A tart with tomatoes during peak season is hard to beat, but the addition of a little Cheddar cheese puts this one over the top.

1 yellow onion

1 tablespoon salted butter, plus more melted for brushing

Salt

1 sheet frozen puff pastry, thawed

2 tablespoons Dijon mustard

⅔ cup grated sharp Cheddar cheese

2 large heirloom tomatoes

Freshly ground black pepper

1. Preheat the oven to 400°F. Line a baking sheet with parchment paper.

2. Slice the onion in half, root to tip, then thinly slice, also root to tip. (This is known as the sauté slice.)

3. In a medium skillet, melt the butter over medium heat. Add the onion and a sprinkle of salt. Cook the onion slowly, stirring only every few minutes, for about 20 minutes, or until very dark and sweet—or caramelized. Remove from the heat. Let cool.

4. Using a rolling pin, lightly roll out the puff pastry, so it is in a rough square shape (it doesn't have to be perfect) of an even thickness and the creases have been smoothed out. Lay the pastry out on the prepared baking sheet. (It's okay if the edges flop over the sides; they will be folded up later.) Paint the inside of the pastry with the Dijon mustard.

5. Spread out the onion over the pastry, leaving a roughly 2-inch border around the edge. Top the onion with the cheese.

6. Cut the tomatoes crosswise into ¼-inch-thick rounds, and arrange on top of the cheese so that they slightly overlap. Sprinkle with salt.

7. Fold up the sides of the pastry over the filling, creating a rustic-looking sheet pan open-face tart. Brush a little melted butter or olive oil over the folded-over pastry edges, and sprinkle with freshly ground black pepper. Drizzle more butter or oil over the tomatoes, and transfer to the oven. Bake for about 30 to 40 minutes, or until golden and puffed. Remove from the oven.

Swap it out: This can also be made in a traditional pie pan. Roll out the dough, and lay it in the pan. You can stack the filling a bit higher and still fold the excess edges over in a rustic style.

Per Serving Calories: 477; Total Fat: 33g; Saturated Fat: 9g; Sodium: 483mg; Carbohydrates: 35g; Fiber: 2g; Sugars: 4g; Protein: 10g

DIVIDE & CONQUER:
Partner 1 can take care of step 1, then move on to slicing and caramelizing the onion while partner 2 rolls out the puff pastry and paints on the mustard. While the onion cools, partner 1 can grate the cheese and slice the tomatoes. Together you can build the tart, fold over the edges, and drizzle with oil.

Walnut-Tarragon Stuffed Mushrooms

GLUTEN-FREE, VEGETARIAN, VEGAN OPTION

Serves 2 / Prep time: 10 minutes / Cook time: 20 minutes

The tarragon is the real standout flavor that makes these stuffed mushrooms special. These stuffed mushrooms are a fantastic meat entrée replacement if you are looking to incorporate more plant-based menu items in your repertoire, and they're also perfect for your favorite vegetarian or vegan pal stopping by.

2 portabella mushrooms

Olive oil, for drizzling

Salt

2 tablespoons salted butter (or coconut oil)

1 cup cremini mushrooms, caps and stems chopped

¼ cup walnuts, finely chopped

2 tablespoons mayonnaise (or vegan mayonnaise)

1 tablespoon chopped fresh tarragon

1. Preheat the oven to 350°F. Line a baking sheet with parchment paper.

2. Scrape out the gills (the black soft feathery underside) of the portabella caps to create space for the filling. Drizzle with oil, and sprinkle with salt. Place the portabellas, scraped-side down, on the prepared baking sheet. Transfer to the oven, and bake for 10 minutes. Remove from the oven, but leave the mushrooms on the baking sheet.

3. While the portabellas are baking, in a medium skillet, melt the butter. Add the cremini mushrooms with a sprinkle of salt, and sauté for about 5 minutes, or until tender. Stir in the walnuts, mayonnaise, and tarragon.

4. Flip the portabella caps over so the scraped side is up. Pile each one high with the sautéed mushroom filling. Drizzle with a little more oil, and bake for 10 minutes. Remove from the oven.

Swap it out: Make mini stuffed mushrooms using cremini (also called baby bella, Roman, or brown) mushrooms instead of large entrée-size portabella mushrooms. These make awesome little hors d'oeuvres for a party.

Per Serving Calories: 339; Total Fat: 34g; Saturated Fat: 10g; Sodium: 166mg; Carbohydrates: 9g; Fiber: 3g; Sugars: 4g; Protein: 7g

DIVIDE & CONQUER: *Partner 1 can take charge of the portabellas in steps 1 and 2 while partner 2 preps the mushroom filling according to the instructions in step 3. Fill the portabella caps together.*

Panfried Chicken with Hot Honey

COMFORT FOOD, GLUTEN-FREE, NUT-FREE

Makes 1 whole chicken (8 pieces) / Prep time: 5 minutes, plus overnight to marinate and 30 minutes to rest / **Cook time:** 30 minutes

When I lived in New York City, there was a restaurant that was open until 4 a.m. where chefs would gather late at night, every night. It had some exquisite offerings, like a raw bar tower with cracked lobster claws and fine oysters, bone marrow, and foie gras, but right there, among all that finery was a dish of fried chicken with warm and spicy honey to drizzle. What have we been doing with our lives that we have not been putting spicy warm honey on fried chicken all this time? The combination is a match made in late-night dining heaven.

For the chicken

1 whole chicken, cut into
    8 pieces
4 cups buttermilk
Salt
Freshly ground
    black pepper
1½ cups rice flour
High-heat oil, for frying

For the hot honey

2 tablespoons honey
1 teaspoon sriracha

To make the chicken

1. Put the chicken in a large zip-top bag. Pour in the buttermilk. Add a few pinches of salt and freshly ground black pepper. Seal the bag, then shake and work the bag so the chicken is all well coated. Refrigerate overnight.

2. Combine the rice flour with several pinches of salt and freshly ground black pepper in a shallow dish, like a pie pan. Pull each piece of chicken out of the buttermilk, and shake off the excess. One by one, dip the chicken pieces into the rice flour, fully coating each piece of chicken. Shake off the excess flour, and put on a baking sheet with a wire rack. Let rest for 20 to 30 minutes.

3. Line a platter with paper towels. Heat about 1½ cups of frying oil in a heavy-bottomed skillet. (There should be enough oil to reach about halfway up the chicken pieces while frying.) When the oil is hot, gently place a piece of

chicken in the skillet at the point furthest from you to avoid splatter. Add another piece or two at a time, with lots of room between pieces so the chicken will brown and crisp but not steam.

4. Adjust the heat as necessary. Once the chicken is added to the skillet, the temperature of the oil drops but will quickly rise after a few minutes. The larger pieces should take 8 to 10 minutes per side. Using tongs, remove the chicken from the oil, and put it on the lined platter. The chicken will continue to cook for a few more minutes after it is removed from the skillet. Insert a meat thermometer into the thickest part of the chicken without hitting the bone (touching the bone will give you an inaccurate reading). The chicken is done when it hits 180°F.

To make the hot honey

5. In a small mixing bowl, combine the honey and sriracha, drizzle over the hot fried chicken, and serve. Gently warm in a small saucepot on the stovetop first, if you'd like.

DIVIDE & CONQUER: *Partner 1 can marinate the chicken while partner 2 makes the hot honey. Together you can dredge the chicken pieces, and, after they rest, fry them.*

Kitchen hack: If you're worried about cooking the chicken all the way through with the panfry method, simply preheat the oven to 375°F, and panfry the chicken on both sides on the stove until golden and crispy. Then place the chicken on a baking sheet fitted with a wire rack (with plenty of space between pieces to avoid steaming) and finish cooking in the oven, about 20 minutes.

Per Serving (4) Calories: 588; Total Fat: 18g; Saturated Fat: 5g; Sodium: 523mg; Carbohydrates: 70g; Fiber: 1g; Sugars: 21g; Protein: 37g

Beef Cabbage Rolls in Creamy Tomato Sauce

COMFORT FOOD, GLUTEN-FREE, NUT-FREE

Serves 4 / Prep time: 30 minutes / Cook time: 2 hours 15 minutes

This dish is a riff off the traditional Polish stuffed cabbage dish called golumpki, *typically made for celebrations like weddings and holidays, but we tend to think it tastes pretty great on any old day. It is warming and tasty and is a bit of a nod to lasagna but not as time-consuming to make. I have made variations in the past by adding different cheeses or vegetables, but my favorite is still the basic version here.*

1 small head
   green cabbage
½ tablespoon
   salted butter
Salt
Freshly ground
   black pepper
8 ounces ground beef
¼ yellow onion
2 (15-ounce)
   cans tomato
   sauce, divided
¼ cup freshly grated
   Parmesan cheese

1. Fill a large stockpot two-thirds full of water. Bring the water to a boil.

2. Core the stem of the cabbage by using a small paring knife and making an angled slice around the stem, then lifting it out and discarding. Peel away any ragged or aging leaves from the outside of the cabbage.

3. Once the water is boiling, add the entire head of cabbage. Let it bob up and down, and flip every so often for about 5 minutes. Using tongs, carefully remove it from the water, and put it on your workspace. Gently peel away the tender cabbage leaves without tearing. (These are the wraps for the rolls.) Repeat boiling and removing the cooked leaves until there is a stack of at least 10 cabbage wraps.

4. Slice the rest of the cabbage thinly. In a large skillet, melt the butter over medium heat. Add the cabbage, and sauté for 3 to 4 minutes, or until soft, then season with salt and pepper. Remove from the heat. Let cool.

5. Preheat the oven to 350°F.

6. Put the beef and sautéed cabbage in a medium mixing bowl. Dice the onion, and add it to the beef. Season with a couple pinches of salt and several turns of freshly ground black pepper. Mix until just combined.

7. Fill the bottom of a 9-by-13-inch casserole dish with 1 can of tomato sauce.

8. Place 2 tablespoons of beef mixture about 1½ inches up from the bottom edge of each cabbage wrap (the edge closest to you), fold the left and right sides toward the middle, then roll the bottom part of the cabbage wrap over the beef and continue rolling away from your body. Place each roll, seam-side down, in the casserole dish.

9. Cover the rolls with the remaining 1 can of tomato sauce, then tightly cover the casserole dish with foil. Transfer to the oven, and bake for 1½ hours. Remove the foil, and bake for 30 more minutes. Remove from the oven. Sprinkle with the Parmesan cheese before serving.

> **DIVIDE & CONQUER:** *Partner 1 can work with the cabbage, completing steps 1 through 4, while partner 2 works on the filling. Together you can fill the rolls and compare who reigns supreme in the cabbage-rolling department. The champion can take over the rolling while the other partner grates the cheese.*

Kitchen hack: If there are leftover boiled cabbage leaves, chop and sauté in butter, add salt and pepper to taste, and you'll have a delicious side dish made from your golumpki scraps.

Per Serving Calories: 246; Total Fat: 8g; Saturated Fat: 2g; Sodium: 1,316mg; Carbohydrates: 26g; Fiber: 7g; Sugars: 14g; Protein: 20g

Skillet Steak and Potatoes with Crispy Sage and Red Wine

DATE NIGHT, GLUTEN-FREE, NUT-FREE

Serves 2 / Prep time: 5 minutes / **Cook time:** 40 minutes

Everyone should have a go-to meat-and-potatoes dish, and this one is mine. I use tenderloin here because, honestly, it is hard to screw up. I also love sirloin and hanger cuts, but with these flavors of red wine, sage, and honey, filets mignons are just right.

2 tablespoons salted butter, divided
2 (4-ounce) filets mignons
Salt
1 cup red wine
2 tablespoons honey
1 tablespoon olive oil
2 medium potatoes, peeled and diced
5 or 6 fresh sage leaves

1. In a large heavy-bottomed skillet, melt 1 tablespoon of butter over medium-high heat. Sprinkle each filet with a large pinch of salt, and sear for 2 to 4 minutes on each side, or until they reach the desired level of doneness. Transfer to a plate or cutting board, and let rest.

2. Deglaze the skillet with the red wine, scraping the bottom to lift off any brown bits left over from the steak. Continue to stir over medium-high heat while drizzling in the honey. Simmer for 10 to 15 minutes, or until the sauce is reduced by half. (If you like a thicker sauce, you can sprinkle in a little arrowroot powder or cornstarch, and whisk the sauce over medium heat until thickened.) Pour the sauce into a small serving bowl.

continued >>

3. Add the remaining 1 tablespoon of butter and the olive oil to the skillet. When the butter and oil are hot, add the potatoes with a large pinch of salt. Cook the potatoes for about 10 minutes, or until crisped on all sides and tender. Add the sage, and let it crisp in the oil. Slice the steak, and add it back to the skillet for 2 to 3 minutes, or just long enough to heat. Remove from the heat.

4. Plate the potatoes and steak. Serve the red wine–honey sauce on the side or drizzled over the steak.

Cooking 101: They say to only cook with wine that you would drink. I do have to agree here. Skip the "cooking wine," and just donate a glass of what you and your partner are drinking that evening to the cause. Alternatively, I have been known to put a cork in a bottle of unfinished wine and keep it in the refrigerator for future cooking; if it was once drinkable, it is acceptable for cooking, in my book.

Per Serving Calories: 524; Total Fat: 12g; Saturated Fat: 6g; Sodium: 133mg; Carbohydrates: 54g; Fiber: 5g; Sugars: 20g; Protein: 29g

DIVIDE & CONQUER:
Partner 1 can prep and salt the steak and get the skillet ready for searing. Partner 2 can prep the rest of the ingredients and chop the potatoes while partner 1 is cooking the steak and reducing the sauce. Partner 2 can rotate in and cook the potatoes while partner 1 plates the steaks.

Panna Cotta with Roasted Strawberries

DATE NIGHT, GLUTEN-FREE, NUT-FREE

Serves 2 / Prep time: 10 minutes, plus 10 minutes to gel and 6 hours or overnight to chill / Cook time: 35 minutes

Panna cotta is a new love of mine. It is one of those desserts that you overlook for years and then you try it and you kick yourself for having ignored it all this time. Another elegant dessert for the repertoire, it's actually just a fancy sort of pudding that whips up quickly and easily. The hardest part is waiting for it to chill overnight before digging in.

1 cup milk, divided

1½ teaspoons unfla-
vored gelatin

¼ cup sugar, plus more
for the strawberries

½ cup yogurt

⅓ cup halved
strawberries

1. Pour 3 tablespoons of milk into a small mixing bowl. Sprinkle with the gelatin, and let sit for 10 minutes.

2. In a small saucepan, bring the remaining milk and the sugar to a simmer over medium heat. Add the gelatin. Stir for 3 to 4 minutes, or until both the sugar and gelatin are completely dissolved. Do not boil.

3. Remove the pan from the heat. Let cool slightly. Whisk in the yogurt.

4. Divide the mixture between 2 glasses or ramekins, cover with plastic wrap, and chill for 6 hours or overnight.

5. About 40 minutes before you are ready to serve the panna cotta, preheat the oven to 350°F. Line a baking sheet with parchment paper. Sprinkle the strawberries with a little sugar, and put them on the prepared baking sheet. Transfer to the oven, and roast for 30 minutes, or until soft. Remove from the oven.

continued >>

6. Top the panna cotta with the strawberries and whatever residual sauce gathers on the baking sheet.

....

Kitchen hack: If you want to invert your panna cottas onto a dish for an extra fancy presentation, butter your glass or ramekin before pouring in the panna cotta mixture. When ready to plate, dip the bottom of the glass in warm water, cover with the serving plate, and swiftly flip over as one unit. Set the plate on the counter, and carefully slip off the glass.

....

Per Serving Calories: 218; Total Fat: 6g; Saturated Fat: 4g; Sodium: 88mg; Carbohydrates: 35g; Fiber: 1g; Sugars: 35g; Protein: 7g

DIVIDE & CONQUER:
Partner 1 can make the gelatin slurry while partner 2 warms the milk and sugar. Partner 2 can continue making the panna cotta while partner 1 gets out the glasses or ramekins and the plastic wrap.

Banana Crème Brûlée

DATE NIGHT, GLUTEN-FREE, NUT-FREE, VEGETARIAN

Serves 2 / Prep time: 5 minutes, plus 6 hours or overnight to chill /
Cook time: 20 minutes

My favorite dessert to make for a dinner party or special occasion is crème brûlée. I am a big fan of shortcuts, and this is definitely one of the easiest ways that I have come across to fake this fancy-schmancy dessert. If you have a torch (hey, some folks do), feel free to skip the broiler and torch the tops. If you're doubling this for a party, let your guests in on the fun by letting them torch their own dessert.

2 large egg yolks

¼ cup sugar, plus more
for sprinkling

1 cup heavy cream

¼ teaspoon vanilla
bean paste

½ cup banana slices

1. Fill a medium saucepan half full of water. Fit a small or medium stainless steel mixing bowl into the saucepan, making sure the bottom of the bowl is not touching the water (or use a double boiler, if you have one).

2. Set the pan on the stovetop over medium-high heat. While waiting for the water to boil, put the egg yolks and sugar in the bowl, and whisk vigorously until the sugar appears to have almost dissolved and the mixture turns pale yellow and glossy.

3. Whisk in the cream. Continue to whisk for 10 to 15 minutes, or until the mixture becomes thick and can coat the back of a spoon.

4. Stir in the vanilla bean paste, and divide the hot vanilla cream between two oven-safe ramekins. Cover with plastic wrap, and refrigerate for 6 hours or overnight.

continued >>

5. About 5 minutes before you are ready to serve the crème brûlée, turn the broiler to high. Arrange the banana slices over the set custards, and sprinkle with a thick and even layer of sugar. Put the ramekins on a baking sheet (for easy handling), and place in the oven about 6 inches below the broiler. Let the sugar bubble and turn a dark golden brown. Remove from the oven. Let cool slightly before enjoying.

Swap it out: Don't like bananas? No problem. Skip them, and just top with a dusting of powdered sugar and a few berries.

Per Serving Calories: 600; Total Fat: 49g; Saturated Fat: 29g; Sodium: 54mg; Carbohydrates: 38g; Fiber: 1g; Sugars: 33g; Protein: 6g

---

DIVIDE & CONQUER:

Partner 1 can set up the saucepan and the bowl while partner 2 gathers and measures all of the ingredients except the banana. Partner 1 can take care of the whisking in steps 2 and 3 while partner 2 pours in the cream. If desired, partner 2 can take over the whisking while partner 1 gets out the ramekins and plastic wrap.

Chocolate Croissant Bread Pudding

COMFORT FOOD, DATE NIGHT, NUT-FREE, VEGETARIAN

Serves 2 / Prep time: 10 minutes / Cook time: 25 minutes

There is no excuse for a bad bread pudding. It should be sweet, moist, and hardly remind you of the plain old bread it once was. I love making bread puddings, but they seldom are made in anything but a giant vat, leaving you to eat bread pudding day in and day out for a week—or beyond, at which point it's way past its prime. These little individual guys are a game changer.

1 cup chocolate chips

1 tablespoon salted butter, plus more for greasing

1 large egg

2 tablespoons sugar, plus more for the whipped cream

½ cup heavy cream, divided

4 croissants, cut into large cubes

1. Preheat the oven to 350°F. Butter two oven-safe ramekins or an 8-by-8-inch baking dish. Put a small mixing bowl in the refrigerator to chill.

2. Fill a medium saucepan half full of water. Fit a small or medium stainless steel mixing bowl into the saucepan, making sure the bottom of the bowl is not touching the water (or use a double boiler, if you have one).

3. Put the chocolate chips and butter in the bowl to melt.

4. In a medium mixing bowl, whisk together the egg and sugar until thick and glossy. Whisk in ¼ cup of cream.

5. Temper the egg mixture by adding the warm melted chocolate a spoonful at a time while whisking, until all of the chocolate has been added.

continued >>

6. Add the croissant pieces to the chocolate mixture, mixing until well saturated. Divide between the ramekins. Transfer to the oven, and bake for 25 minutes, or until the top is shiny and the inside is soft but not runny. Remove from the oven.

7. In the chilled small mixing bowl, whip the remaining ¼ cup of cream and a sprinkle of sugar by whisking vigorously.

8. Top the bread puddings with the whipped cream, and enjoy.

Prep tip: If the bread pudding batter does not look very well saturated, go ahead and add more cream to the chocolate croissant mix. Opt for more liquid over not enough. You want to be sure that the mix is quite wet but not runny. Don't worry—there are eggs in there, so it will set up just great; remember, it does not need to be as firm as a traditional cake.

Per Serving Calories: 1,312; Total Fat: 84g; Saturated Fat: 48g; Sodium: 986mg; Carbohydrates: 139g; Fiber: 3g; Sugars: 91g; Protein: 22g

DIVIDE & CONQUER:

Partner 1 can preheat the oven and melt the chocolate as directed in steps 1 through 3 while partner 2 chops or tears the croissant and whisks together the eggs, sugar, and cream. Together, temper the egg mixture with the chocolate so you have accountability if it curdles. Partner 1 can continue with step 6 while partner 2 whips the cream.

Red Berry Marbled Macaroons

DAIRY-FREE, GLUTEN-FREE, VEGETARIAN

Makes 10 cookies / Prep time: 5 minutes / Cook time: 30 minutes

Whenever I see plain old coconut macaroons on a platter at a party, I have to say, I'm not excited. I need some chocolate on the bottom or drizzled on top or just something a little extra. This variation has a jammy ribbon that is just enough flourish to the standard ol' coconut blob of a cookie to entice me. I love these little guys. They are no longer boring, and a little pink and a tart raspberry flavor go nicely with the traditional rich coconut flavor.

2 large egg whites

2 teaspoons honey

½ teaspoon
    almond extract

Pinch salt

7 ounces sweetened
    shredded coconut

2 tablespoons
    raspberry jam

1. Preheat the oven to 350°F. Line a baking sheet with parchment paper.

2. In a medium mixing bowl, whisk together the egg whites, honey, almond extract, and salt. Add the coconut and mix until incorporated.

3. Add the raspberry jam. Stir just enough to create jammy ribbons throughout the coconut mixture.

4. Drop scoops from a ¾-inch-diameter ice cream scoop, or about 2 teaspoons, onto the prepared baking sheet. Transfer to the oven, and bake for 25 to 30 minutes, or until deep golden on the bottom. Remove from the oven.

continued »

Kitchen hack: If you would like a chocolatey drizzle across the top of these cookies, melt a little chocolate, and let it cool just slightly. Then, using a rubber spatula, scrape the chocolate into a zip-top bag, work the chocolate into a corner, and snip the tiniest hole in the corner. You now have a piping bag to drizzle a few stripes of chocolate across the top of each macaroon.

Per Serving (1 cookie) Calories: 65; Total Fat: 4g; Saturated Fat: 3g; Sodium: 39mg; Carbohydrates: 7g; Fiber: 1g; Sugars: 7g; Protein: 1g

DIVIDE & CONQUER:

Partner 1 can take care of steps 1 and 2 while partner 2 gets the coconut and jam measured out. Partner 1 can mix in the coconut, and partner 2 can spoon in the jam as partner 1 continues to stir. Together, you can scoop cookies onto the prepared baking sheet.

Dark Chocolate-Covered Strawberries

DATE NIGHT, DAIRY-FREE, GLUTEN-FREE, NUT-FREE, VEGAN

Makes 6 large strawberries / Prep time: 5 minutes, plus 10 minutes to chill / Cook time: 5 minutes

It is so fun to see chocolate-covered strawberries around Valentine's Day or in fancy chocolate shops, but it is surprising that more people don't make them at home, since they are so fun to make together, take very little skill, and have a great payoff. Get extra fancy by melting some white chocolate on the side to double-dip your berries, or roll them in chopped nuts, mini chocolate chips, or coconut flakes. Aside from being a romantic treat for two, they also make for great little sweets to box up as gifts for others.

1 (3-ounce) bar dark chocolate

6 large strawberries, preferably with the stems

1. Line a plate or small baking sheet with parchment paper.

2. Break the chocolate bar into pieces, and put them in a small skillet over very low heat. Allow the chocolate to melt very slowly, using a rubber spatula to stir.

3. Once the chocolate is melted and smooth, remove from the heat. Dip each strawberry into it, rolling the strawberry around to coat it thickly. Let excess chocolate drip off, and put each dipped strawberry on the prepared plate. Refrigerate for about 10 minutes, or until the chocolate firms up.

continued >>

Ingredient tip: Typically, around Valentine's Day is when you will see the large strawberries with the long pretty stem attached; these are not necessary but nice to have. You can also dip dried apricots or bananas on a stick to make banana pops.

Per Serving (1 strawberry) Calories: 66; Total Fat: 4g; Saturated Fat: 3g; Sodium: 5mg; Carbohydrates: 9g; Fiber: 1g; Sugars: 7g; Protein: 1g

---

DIVIDE & CONQUER:
Partner 1 can prepare the plate, and partner 2 can melt the chocolate. Together, try your hand at dipping the strawberries into the chocolate (it's fun!).

*Hoisin Pork Lettuce Cups with
Savory Carrot Slaw, page 160*

One-Pot

Cheesy Sausage and Tomato Frittata

GLUTEN-FREE, NUT-FREE

Serves 2 to 4 / Prep time: 5 minutes / **Cook time:** 25 minutes

A frittata is basically a crustless quiche, and it's a cinch to throw together. I love a frittata. Just about anything can go into this lovely, one-skillet breakfast hit as long as you have a few eggs in the house. Whenever the refrigerator is running empty—perhaps with just a lonely scallion, one slice of Swiss cheese, and some spinach that's nearing its last days, a frittata always is the perfect solution. This particular cheese, sausage, and tomato combination is delicious for when you have guests for brunch; just double the recipe and use a bigger skillet. Pair with a simple Bibb lettuce salad and some mimosas, and you have yourself a breakfast of champions.

5 ounces
  ground sausage
1 tablespoon
  salted butter
¼ cup diced
  yellow onion
½ cup halved cherry
  tomatoes
6 large eggs
Salt
Freshly ground
  black pepper
½ cup shredded
  Cheddar cheese

1. Preheat the oven to 350°F.

2. In a small oven-safe skillet, brown the sausage over medium heat. When the sausage has browned, add the butter, onion, and tomatoes. Sauté for 10 minutes, or until the onion has caramelized and the tomatoes have softened and slightly browned.

3. Whisk the eggs until very well combined. Season with a large pinch of salt and several turns of freshly ground black pepper, then pour the eggs into the skillet over the sausage and vegetables. Sprinkle the cheese on top. Turn off the heat, and transfer to the oven.

4. Cook for 15 minutes, or until the eggs have just set. Remove from the oven.

....

Swap it out: Other favorite vegetarian combinations include mushroom and Gruyère, or spinach and feta. Always add caramelized onions to a frittata—they go with every combination.

....

Per Serving Calories: 605; Total Fat: 46g; Saturated Fat: 20g; Sodium: 1,038mg; Carbohydrates: 7g; Fiber: 1g; Sugars: 4g; Protein: 38g

---

DIVIDE & CONQUER:

Partner 1 can preheat the oven, brown the sausage, and cook the onion and tomatoes in step 2, and partner 2 can complete steps 3 and 4, whisking the eggs and finishing the frittata.

Green Shakshuka

GLUTEN-FREE OPTION, NUT-FREE, VEGETARIAN

Serves 2 / Prep time: 5 minutes / Cook time: 10 minutes

My partner and I were in Israel for a friend's wedding the first time we enjoyed shakshuka, and we must have ordered this dish 9 times in 10 days. Shakshuka is made with Middle Eastern or North African spices, savory tomato sauce, and eggs, all simmered together in one skillet. When we got home, we were jonesing for shakshuka, and I took the liberty of riffing off the classic. With a few pieces of hearty toast, this dish is a forever favorite.

2 tablespoons
   salted butter
½ cup heavy cream
2 cups fresh spinach
Salt
Freshly ground
   black pepper
½ cup crumbled
   feta cheese
4 large eggs
Toast, for serving
   (optional)

1. In a small skillet, melt the butter over medium heat. Add the cream, spinach, a large pinch of salt, and several turns of freshly ground black pepper. Stir for 1 to 2 minutes, or until the spinach has wilted, then sprinkle on the feta cheese.

2. Use a large spoon to create 4 shallow dips in the surface of the spinach mixture. Crack the eggs one at a time into each hollow, leaving plenty of room between them. Season each yolk with salt, and add a fitted lid to the skillet. Reduce the heat to low, and simmer for about 5 minutes, or until the egg whites have cooked and the yolks are still runny. Remove from the heat. Serve with the toast (if using).

Kitchen hack: To ensure that the egg yolks do not break in the pan, crack each egg into a small dish or ramekin first, then pour it gently into the skillet (you can use the same small dish; just crack and add the eggs one at a time).

Per Serving Calories: 557; Total Fat: 51g; Saturated Fat: 30g; Sodium: 689mg; Carbohydrates: 5g; Fiber: 1g; Sugars: 4g; Protein: 20g

DIVIDE & CONQUER:
Partner 1 can measure out the ingredients, make the toast (if using), and set the table while partner 2 cooks the shakshuka.

Puff Pastry Eggs with Prosciutto and Cheese

NUT-FREE, VEGETARIAN OPTION

Makes 4 pastries / **Prep time:** 15 minutes / **Cook time:** 25 minutes

I used to walk a mile to the most fabulous bakery, Breadfarm in Edison, Washington, for the most fantastic savory puff pastry eggs. When we moved away, I tried my hand at these puffy, salty, hammy, little egg squares, and it was a roaring success. These elegant little bites—with crispy edges of flakey pastry and a soft-baked egg with cheese and crisp cured ham in the center— look impressive but are actually quite simple. I no longer need to walk a mile to have them. But I would.

1 sheet frozen puff
    pastry, thawed
Butter, for greasing
4 large eggs
½ cup shredded
    Cheddar cheese
2 strips prosciutto
    (optional)
Salt
Freshly ground
    black pepper
Fresh thyme (optional)

1. Preheat the oven to 400°F. Line a baking sheet with parchment paper.

2. Using a rolling pin, lightly roll out the puff pastry, so it is in a rough square shape (it doesn't have to be perfect) of an even thickness and the creases have been smoothed out. Cut the dough into fourths, slicing in half once lengthwise and once crosswise.

3. Put each piece of pastry on the prepared baking sheet. Grease or butter the outside bottom of four oven-safe ramekins or any small oven-safe dish, and place one in the middle of each piece of pastry. Transfer the baking sheet to the oven. Bake the pastries with the ramekins sitting in the middle for 10 minutes, or until the edges have puffed up around the ramekins, creating a well for each egg. Remove the baking sheet from the oven, and, using hot pads or oven mitts, remove the ramekins.

4. Gently crack an egg into the center of each pastry, in the hollows formed by the ramekins, and sprinkle each with the cheese and a few pieces of torn prosciutto (if using). Season each with a pinch of salt and freshly ground black pepper.

5. Transfer the baking sheet to the oven, and bake for 15 to 20 minutes, or until the eggs are cooked to your liking. Remove from the oven. Top with thyme (if using).

Swap it out: For a vegetarian flavor variation, try sliced baby tomatoes, some pesto, and plenty of freshly grated Parmesan cheese on top.

Per Serving (1 pastry) Calories: 938; Total Fat: 66g; Saturated Fat: 16g; Sodium: 632mg; Carbohydrates: 58g; Fiber: 2g; Sugars: 1g; Protein: 28g

DIVIDE & CONQUER:
Partner 1 can complete steps 1 through 3, rolling out, cutting, and preparing the pastry. Partner 2 can take over in step 4, cracking in the eggs, sprinkling the cheese, and tearing the prosciutto.

Cream of Zucchini Soup with Cumin and Coriander

GLUTEN-FREE, NUT-FREE, VEGETARIAN

Makes about 3 cups / Prep time: 5 minutes / Cook time: 20 minutes

I always say I have three major cooking role models: my mother for sourcing ingredients and her knowledge of nutrition, my friend Ashley's mother for all-American, balanced meals full of clean flavors, and my friend Simone's mother—Mama Adrienne—whose style is what I like to call French farm-house chic. As kids, we would sit on Mama Adrienne's counter, eating chilled roasted asparagus dipped in creamy hollandaise or spooning bouillabaisse out of Tupperware. She made the most exquisite things with such ease. This recipe is based off a one-pot cream of zucchini soup that she made. It is one of my most delicious memories . . . and it is so elegantly simple.

1 tablespoon
　　salted butter
1 garlic clove, chopped
¼ yellow onion, chopped
2 zucchini, chopped
1 cup vegetable broth
1 cup heavy cream
½ teaspoon salt
Pinch ground cumin
Pinch ground coriander
Freshly ground
　　black pepper

1. In a medium stockpot, melt the butter over medium heat. Add the garlic and onion. Sauté for about 5 minutes, or until translucent.

2. Add the zucchini and broth. Simmer for about 5 minutes, or until the zucchini is soft.

3. Use an immersion blender, or let cool slightly and pour into a countertop blender. Blend until smooth. (If using a standing blender, return the soup to the pot.)

4. Add the cream, salt, cumin, coriander, and pepper. Simmer over medium-low heat for about 10 minutes. Remove from the heat.

Swap it out: Use chicken broth instead of vegetable broth for a slightly richer soup. Yellow summer squash will also work well in place of zucchini.

Per Serving (1 cup) Calories: 342; Total Fat: 34g; Saturated Fat: 21g; Sodium: 636mg; Carbohydrates: 10g; Fiber: 2g; Sugars: 6g; Protein: 4g

---

DIVIDE & CONQUER:
Partner 1 can organize, chop, and measure out the ingredients for partner 2, who can make the soup.

Corn and Crab Chowder

GLUTEN-FREE, NUT-FREE

Serves 4 / Prep time: 10 minutes / Cook time: 25 minutes

We are big fans of crab. This chowder has a great little kick, with the salty and delicate crab and sweet corn to drive it home. We often make a double batch and freeze the extra portions for later. This chowder is hearty enough on its own as an entrée or makes for a great lunch accompanied by a salad. We use fresh corn in the summer and frozen in the winter. I have also tried swapping out the cream for full-fat coconut milk and adding a little bit of ancho chile powder, lime juice, and fresh cilantro on top, just to change things up once in a while.

1 tablespoon salted butter

½ cup chopped onion

1 celery stalk, chopped

1 large Yukon gold potato, peeled and finely diced

1½ teaspoons Old Bay seasoning

1 teaspoon salt

2 cups vegetable stock

1 cup frozen corn

8 ounces lump crab

½ cup heavy cream

1 tablespoon chopped fresh parsley

1. In a heavy-bottomed medium stockpot or Dutch oven, melt the butter over medium-high heat. Add the onion, celery, and potato. Sauté for 5 minutes, or until the onion and celery have begun to soften and the potatoes have slightly browned.

2. Add the Old Bay seasoning, salt, and stock. Bring to a simmer. Cook for about 20 minutes, or until the potatoes have softened.

3. Add the corn, crab, and cream. Stir, taste, and adjust the seasoning, if needed. Remove from the heat. Sprinkle with the parsley for garnish.

Cooking 101: To freeze, cool the soup down quickly by removing the pot from the heat and setting the entire thing in an ice bath while stirring to help release heat. Store flat in large freezer-safe zip-top bags. Label with the recipe name and the date. This chowder can stay frozen for up to 3 months.

Per Serving Calories: 295; Total Fat: 15g; Saturated Fat: 9g; Sodium: 1,353mg; Carbohydrates: 24g; Fiber: 3g; Sugars: 6g; Protein: 18g

DIVIDE & CONQUER:

Partner 1 can chop and measure out all of the ingredients, and partner 2 can complete steps 1 and 2, sautéing the vegetables, simmering, and seasoning the chowder. Partner 1 can jump back in at step 3 and add the finishing touches.

Smoky Tomato-Lentil Stew

DAIRY-FREE, GLUTEN-FREE, VEGAN

Serves 6 / Prep time: 15 minutes / Cook time: 45 minutes

This is my very favorite stew. My husband, my clients, my mom—we just can't get enough. Lentils had never been in my top ten until I came up with this stew, and now I crave lentils. I just can't get enough! This recipe is simple and very satisfying to make with your sweetie. Lots of chopping is called for, but you don't need Michelin-star knife skills—just keep the vegetables all roughly the same size so they cook evenly. Feel free to taste and adjust the seasoning as you go. (I like to use the slightly spicier Madras curry powder, but use whatever curry powder you like.) Soups tend to taste even better the next day, and the day after that, so make a double batch, and you can enjoy it all week.

2 tablespoons
   coconut oil
¼ yellow onion, chopped
1 celery stalk, chopped
1 red bell
   pepper, chopped
1 small sweet
   potato, chopped
1 small yellow
   potato, chopped
1 large carrot, chopped
1½ teaspoons
   curry powder
¼ cup white wine
½ cup green
   lentils, rinsed

1. In a heavy-bottomed medium stockpot or Dutch oven, heat the coconut oil over medium-high heat. Add the onion, celery, bell pepper, sweet potato, yellow potato, and carrot. Sauté for 3 to 4 minutes.

2. Add the curry powder, stir, then add the wine.

3. Add the lentils, tomatoes, stock, coconut milk, and salt. Stir, and simmer for 30 to 40 minutes, or until the lentils are soft and the potatoes are tender. Taste, and adjust the seasoning, if needed. Remove from the heat.

1 (15-ounce) can
    fire-roasted
    tomatoes
1 cup vegetable stock
1 (13½-ounce) can
    coconut milk
1 teaspoon salt

Ingredient tip: There are four main types of lentils and several specialty varieties. Green or brown lentils may be used interchangeably for this recipe. Red and yellow lentils will break down too quickly. Always rinse lentils, and pick through them to remove any debris, stones, or shriveled bits before use.

Per Serving Calories: 285; Total Fat: 17g; Saturated Fat: 14g; Sodium: 714mg; Carbohydrates: 26g; Fiber: 8g; Sugars: 6g; Protein: 7g

---

DIVIDE & CONQUER:

Chop the vegetables together. Then partner 1 can begin cooking the vegetables as directed in step 1 while partner 2 measures the remaining ingredients and adds them in the order directed in steps 2 and 3.

Faux Pho

DAIRY-FREE, GLUTEN-FREE, NUT-FREE, VEGETARIAN, VEGAN OPTION

Serves 2 / **Prep time:** 10 minutes / **Cook time:** 15 minutes

Pho is a popular Vietnamese soup that can be found in restaurants around the world, from street carts to high-end dining establishments. Pho consists of a savory broth, rice noodles, herbs, and (usually) meat. This recipe takes a shortcut by using miso to achieve the delicious, umami layers of flavor that are reminiscent of a proper pho broth—which is traditionally simmered for hours upon hours. If you're not committed to making a vegetarian pho, feel free to swap out the vegetable stock for beef or chicken stock to further deepen the flavors of this faux pho.

2 ounces glass noodles

3 cups vegetable stock

3 tablespoons red miso

1 carrot

1 zucchini

¼ red onion

5 shiitake mushrooms

2 garlic cloves

10 snow peas or green beans

1 teaspoon minced ginger

¼ cup tamari

1 tablespoon honey (or maple syrup)

1 teaspoon sriracha (or favorite hot sauce)

1 scallion, green and white parts, chopped

1 radish, thinly sliced

1. Put the glass noodles in a medium mixing bowl, and add boiled water to cover. Let cook for 2 to 3 minutes, or until soft. Drain, and rinse very well with cold water to stop the cooking and remove excess starches.

2. In a medium stockpot, stir together the stock and miso. Bring to a simmer.

3. Cut the carrot and zucchini into matchsticks, and thinly slice the onion, mushrooms, and garlic. Add to the pot. Add the snow peas, ginger, tamari, honey, and sriracha. Simmer for about 10 minutes, or until the vegetables are just tender. Add the noodles. Remove from the heat.

½ cup mung bean
    sprouts, divided
¼ cup fresh cilan-
    tro leaves
5 fresh mint leaves
5 fresh basil leaves
1 soft-boiled large egg
    (optional)
1 sheet nori (optional)

4. Divide the soup between two serving bowls. Top with the scallion, radish, sprouts, and cilantro. Tear the mint and basil, and sprinkle them on top. Peel the soft-boiled egg and slice it in half (if using), and add half to each bowl. Crunch up the nori sheet (if using), and sprinkle on top of each bowl.

Cooking 101: If making this soup in advance, keep the rice noodles separate rather than adding them to the soup. Prepare the noodles just before serving, and add them to each person's bowls right before enjoying.

Per Serving Calories: 294; Total Fat: 1g; Saturated Fat: <1g; Sodium: 3,666mg; Carbohydrates: 61g; Fiber: 5g; Sugars: 21g; Protein: 13g

---

DIVIDE & CONQUER:
Partner 1 can do steps 1 and 2, while partner 2 takes care of step 3, chopping the vegetables and assembling the soup. Complete step 4 together.

Thai Curry Butternut Squash Soup

DAIRY-FREE, GLUTEN-FREE, VEGETARIAN

Serves 2 / Prep time: 10 minutes / Cook time: 20 minutes

In the season when golden gourds are abundant and every restaurant has a butternut squash ravioli or soup, try your hand at this Thai curry version to shake things up. I serve this soup as a first course at my own family's Thanksgiving dinner, but it is so quick and simple to whip up that you can enjoy it all autumn long. Sweet and smooth butternut squash? Flavorful and slightly sweet and spicy Thai curry with creamy coconut milk and lime? Yes, yes, a thousand times yes.

1 tablespoon coconut oil

¼ yellow onion, chopped

1 cup butternut
    squash chunks

1 teaspoon red Thai
    curry paste

1 tablespoon tamari

Juice of ½ lime

1 cup vegetable stock

1 (13½-ounce) can
    coconut milk

1 teaspoon honey

¼ teaspoon salt

1. In a medium stockpot, heat the oil over medium-high heat.

2. Add the onion and squash. Sauté for about 5 minutes.

3. Add the Thai curry paste, tamari, lime juice, stock, coconut milk, honey, and salt. Simmer for 15 minutes, or until the squash is fork-tender. Remove from the heat.

4. Use an immersion blender, or let cool slightly and pour into a countertop blender. Blend until smooth. Taste, and adjust the seasoning, if needed.

Ingredient tip: Winter squash are abundant in the fall and store well through the winter (hence the name). They can all be used in this soup, including butternut, delicata, kabocha, and acorn—truly any golden variety you see.

Per Serving Calories: 490; Total Fat: 42g; Saturated Fat: 36g; Sodium: 1,218mg; Carbohydrates: 22g; Fiber: 3g; Sugars: 10g; Protein: 6g

DIVIDE & CONQUER:

Partner 1 can measure out the ingredients, and partner 2 can make the soup.

Stuffed Spaghetti Squash Lasagna

COMFORT FOOD, GLUTEN-FREE, NUT-FREE, VEGETARIAN

Serves 2 / **Prep time:** 5 minutes / **Cook time:** 50 minutes

All the flavors of lasagna without the hours of work? Sign me up. The best part of this dish is the built-in squash bowl. A straightforward procedure of scooping it out, mixing it up, stuffing it back in, and baking makes this dish easy enough to pull off when you are tired, home late, and starving. Or just when you want to have something amazing. You each get your own half-squash to eat from, making for easy eating at the table or parked on the couch. Mix in cooked ground beef if you prefer a Bolognese-style lasagna—and feel free to add extra basil and Parmesan, as we do.

1 spaghetti squash

Avocado oil, for coating

Salt

Freshly ground
    black pepper

½ to 1 cup tomato sauce

½ cup ricotta cheese

½ cup freshly grated
    Parmesan cheese

1 (8-ounce) ball fresh
    mozzarella

4 or 5 basil leaves

1. Preheat the oven to 375°F. Line a baking sheet with parchment paper.

2. Halve the squash, stem to root, and place, cut-side down, on the prepared baking sheet. Rub with a little oil so the squash is coated, and transfer to the oven. Roast for about 30 minutes, or until soft. Remove from the oven.

3. Let the squash cool before handling. Flip the squash over on the baking sheet, and gently scoop out and discard the seeds. Using a fork, lift out the squash strands into a large mixing bowl. Season generously with salt and freshly ground black pepper.

4. Gently stir in the tomato sauce, ricotta, and Parmesan cheese. Fill each squash shell with the squash, tomato, and cheese mixture. Tear the fresh mozzarella into pieces, and arrange on top of each half squash. Return the baking sheet to the oven, and bake for 20 minutes, or until the cheese has melted. Remove from the oven. Tear the basil, and sprinkle on top before serving.

....

Mix it up: For another flavor profile, try pesto instead of tomatoes, with chopped cherry tomatoes and some pine nuts.

....

Per Serving Calories: 672; Total Fat: 37g; Saturated Fat: 21g; Sodium: 1,282mg; Carbohydrates: 32g; Fiber: 6g; Sugars: 12g; Protein: 42g

DIVIDE & CONQUER:
Partner 1 can begin with steps 1 and 2. Scoop out the squash together. Then partner 2 can mix up the filling while partner 1 tears up the mozzarella and basil.

Skillet Sherry Chicken Thighs and Maple-Orange Roasted Roots

COMFORT FOOD, DATE NIGHT, DAIRY-FREE, GLUTEN-FREE, NUT-FREE

Serves 2 / Prep time: 10 minutes / Cook time: 50 minutes

Most comfort food is thought of as heavy, cheesy, and rich. I typically think of macaroni and cheese, a loaded baked potato, brownies, and the like. All very tasty and delicious, of course, if not very good for you. Thankfully, this one-skillet meal manages to be the coziest and most comforting dish in my arsenal—without sacrificing the nutrition. Casual enough for you and your honey but also elegant enough for guests or when you want something a little special for a date night in. Change up the root vegetables to suit your taste: Carrots, parsnips, or fingerling potatoes all work for this homey meal.

4 bone-in, skin-on
   chicken thighs
Salt
1 carrot
1 parsnip
1 small sweet potato
1 small red onion
Zest and juice of
   1 orange
1 tablespoon olive oil
2 tablespoons
   maple syrup
1 teaspoon mustard
Freshly ground
   black pepper

1. Preheat the oven to 350°F.

2. Rinse and pat the chicken thighs dry. Season the skin of each thigh with plenty of salt.

3. Heat a large oven-safe heavy-bottomed skillet over medium-high heat. Lay the thighs skin-side down with plenty of room between pieces so they brown well. Cook for 5 to 7 minutes, or until the skin is dark golden and crisp. Flip, and cook for just a few minutes on the other side.

4. While the thighs are browning, chop the carrot, parsnip, and sweet potato into large bite-size chunks. (Cutting the roots to a similar size will ensure that they cook more evenly.) Cut the onion into thick wedges.

5. Transfer the chicken to a plate. Add the carrot, parsnip, sweet potato, and onion to the skillet. Sauté for a few minutes, then season with salt and several turns of freshly ground black pepper. Add the orange zest and juice, olive oil, maple syrup, and mustard. Season with pepper. Stir until the vegetables are well coated. Place the chicken, skin-side up, atop the vegetables, and transfer to the oven.

6. Cook for about 35 minutes, or until the vegetables are fork-tender and the chicken is cooked through. Remove from the oven.

Cooking 101: For nice and evenly crispy skin, be sure to pat the skin very dry. Not only will excess water or liquid inhibit browning, but also it will make hot oil pop and spatter.

Per Serving Calories: 780; Total Fat: 46g; Saturated Fat: 11g; Sodium: 68mg; Carbohydrates: 54g; Fiber: 7g; Sugars: 23g; Protein: 41g

DIVIDE & CONQUER:

Partner 1 can complete steps 1 through 3 while partner 2 chops the vegetables. After partner 1 transfers the chicken to a plate, partner 2 can cook the vegetables and finish the recipe.

Chicken Paprikash

COMFORT FOOD, GLUTEN-FREE, NUT-FREE

Serves 2 / Prep time: 5 minutes / Cook time: 45 minutes

This Hungarian paprika chicken dish is the epitome of comfort food. Serving it over potatoes, egg noodles, or rice (although nontraditional) really pulls this dish together. Paprika can have a variety of flavor profiles, from mild and sweet to spicy or even smoky. Paprika is rising in popularity among chefs and home cooks alike. You may have a jar in your spice rack that you once used to top deviled eggs, and it probably tastes like sawdust by now, so go ahead and grab a fresh bottle before you embark on your chicken paprikash mission. Chicken breast is lean and tends to dry out unless cooked perfectly, so I opt for bone-in, skin-on pieces—they are more forgiving, especially in one-pot meals.

1½ pounds
    bone-in, skin-on
    chicken breasts
1 tablespoon
    salted butter
1 yellow onion, sliced
Salt
Freshly ground
    black pepper
1 tablespoon Hungarian
    paprika
¼ teaspoon spicy
    paprika or cayenne
½ cup chicken broth
⅓ cup sour cream

1. Heat a large heavy-bottomed skillet over medium-high heat. Place the chicken in the skillet, skin-side down, and brown for 5 to 7 minutes, or until golden and crispy. Flip, and cook for 1 to 2 minutes. Transfer the chicken to a plate.

2. Put the butter in the same skillet. When it has melted, add the onion, and cook for about 5 minutes, or until softened. Sprinkle with a large pinch of salt and a few turns of freshly ground black pepper.

3. Add the Hungarian paprika and spicy paprika. Stir to coat the onion. Sauté for 5 minutes.

4. Add the broth, and scrape up the brown bits on the bottom. Put the chicken pieces back in the skillet, and cover. Cook the chicken for 20 to 25 minutes, or until cooked through.

continued »

5. Remove the chicken one more time. Stir in the sour cream, then add the chicken back in. Taste and adjust the seasoning, if needed. Remove from the heat.

Mix it up: Some delicious additions would be sliced red bell pepper that can be added in with the onions and lots of chopped fresh parsley, for topping the dish.

Per Serving Calories: 765; Total Fat: 46g; Saturated Fat: 19g; Sodium: 518mg; Carbohydrates: 10g; Fiber: 2g; Sugars: 6g; Protein: 74g

> **DIVIDE & CONQUER:**
> *Partner 1 can slice the onion and get the ingredients measured out in order. Partner 2 can cook the chicken while partner 1 prepares a simple side of boiled or mashed potatoes, egg noodles, or rice.*

Roasted Chicken over Peasant Bread with Fingerlings (aka Million-Dollar Chicken)

DATE NIGHT, NUT-FREE

Serves 2, with leftovers / Prep time: 10 minutes, plus overnight for the crème fraîche to set up / Cook time: 1 hour 40 minutes

If you are in the market for a signature dish, look no further. I know this dish as "Million-Dollar Chicken." It is one of the most fun dishes I have ever made, and to this day it's my most-requested dish from family and friends. It is truly a head-turner, with luxurious crème fraîche–basted chicken roasted over crusty bread, infusing it with tons of flavor.

1 cup heavy cream

⅓ cup buttermilk

1 teaspoon minced shallot

½ teaspoon grated lemon zest

Salt

2 or 3 thick-crusted bread slices

½ cup olive oil, divided

1 whole chicken, cleaned and patted dry, giblets removed

10 fingerling potatoes, quartered lengthwise

1. To make the crème fraîche, in a glass bowl (I use my favorite Pyrex), combine the cream and buttermilk, cover loosely with plastic wrap, and set in a nondrafty, warm spot overnight. The oven (turned off), a kitchen cabinet, or the microwave are all good places to let the cream set up. The next morning, stir the crème fraîche, cover it, and refrigerate.

2. When you are ready to cook the chicken, stir the shallot and lemon zest into the crème fraîche along with a large pinch of salt.

3. Preheat the oven to 375°F.

4. On a baking sheet, lay out the bread, and brush both sides with olive oil. Arrange the bread so the chicken can sit on top. Truss the chicken by using kitchen twine to tie the legs together. Place the chicken on top of the bread, and season generously with salt.

continued »

5. Scatter the potatoes around the bread, and drizzle with the remaining olive oil and a large pinch of salt. Brush the chicken with about one-third of the crème fraîche. It's okay—preferable, even—if it drips down onto the bread and potatoes. Transfer the baking sheet to the oven, and roast for 1 hour. Remove from the oven.

6. Using tongs and a spatula for assistance, transfer the chicken from the bread to a large plate. Flip the bread slices over. Don't worry if the bread is very dark; that is perfect. Place the chicken on top of the flipped bread, and brush with another third of the crème fraîche. Return to the oven, roast for 20 minutes, then remove from the oven, and brush with the remaining third of crème fraîche.

7. Return the baking sheet to the oven, and roast for 20 minutes, or until the chicken and potatoes have cooked through. Remove from the oven. Insert a meat thermometer into the thickest part of the chicken thigh without hitting the bone. The temperature should read 165°F when the chicken is done.

8. Serve the chicken on a platter with the roasted bread and fingerling potatoes.

....

Kitchen hack: Don't feel like having the whole bird? Look for a bone-in, skin-on chicken breast and a couple of drumsticks. The presentation will not be the same as a whole roasted chicken, but you will not have to worry about having too many leftovers or carving the chicken.

....

Per Serving Calories: 1,641; Total Fat: 130g; Saturated Fat: 43g; Sodium: 985mg; Carbohydrates: 60g; Fiber: 4g; Sugars: 10g; Protein: 64g

DIVIDE & CONQUER:

Either partner can make the crème fraîche the night before. On the day of cooking, partner 1 can cut the potatoes and complete steps 2 and 3 while partner 2 prepares the bread and chicken according to the directions in step 4. Partner 1 can scatter the potatoes while partner 2 brushes on the crème fraîche. Work together to complete steps 6 through 8.

Hoisin Pork Lettuce Cups with Savory Carrot Slaw

DAIRY-FREE, GLUTEN-FREE OPTION, NUT-FREE

Serves 2 / Prep time: 15 minutes / Cook time: 15 minutes

Lettuce cups are crunchy, light, and satisfying. It's important that they have an incredible filling with lots of umami flavor. Thick, sweet, and savory hoisin sauce complements the ground pork and, with the addition of garlic and ginger, makes this dish lip-smackingly divine. Swap out the pork for ground chicken or chopped shrimp for a change, and look for gluten-free hoisin sauce, if needed.

2 teaspoons sesame oil, divided

¼ cup chopped yellow onion

½ teaspoon minced garlic

½ teaspoon minced shallot

½ teaspoon minced ginger

8 ounces ground pork

1½ teaspoons rice vinegar

Juice of 1 lime, divided

1 tablespoon hoisin sauce (or gluten-free hoisin sauce)

Pinch red pepper flakes

6 whole Bibb lettuce leaves

1 carrot, grated

1. In a large skillet, heat 1½ teaspoons of sesame oil over medium heat. Add the onion. Sauté for 3 to 4 minutes, or until soft. Add the garlic, shallot, ginger, and pork. Break up the pork, and cook for 7 to 10 minutes, or until browned.

2. Add the vinegar, juice of ½ lime, the hoisin sauce, and red pepper flakes. Remove from the heat.

3. Fill each lettuce cup with about one-sixth of the ground pork.

4. Top each lettuce cup with a tiny pile of carrot, radish, scallion, and sesame seeds, then finish with a small drizzle of the remaining ½ teaspoon of sesame oil and juice of ½ lime. Season with salt.

1 radish, thinly sliced

1 scallion, green and
white parts, chopped

¼ teaspoon black
sesame seeds

Salt

Mix it up: Ever try water chestnuts? Pick up a small can at the grocery store, and add a few chopped water chestnuts to the pork. A few torn leaves of Thai basil are also a nice addition. The water chestnuts provide a crunchy texture to the filling, and the Thai basil has a distinct flavor, a brighter and slightly more licorice-y flavor that pairs perfectly with the other ingredients.

Per Serving Calories: 399; Total Fat: 29g; Saturated Fat: 10g; Sodium: 220mg; Carbohydrates: 11g; Fiber: 2g; Sugars: 6g; Protein: 21g

DIVIDE & CONQUER:

Partner 1 can get the ingredients together while partner 2 cooks the pork filling. Assemble the lettuce cups together.

Stuffed Meat Loaf with Spicy Roasted Cauliflower

COMFORT FOOD, DAIRY-FREE, GLUTEN-FREE OPTION, NUT-FREE

Serves 4 / **Prep time:** 15 minutes / **Cook time:** 1 hour

The '50s grayish log of mystery meat formerly known as meat loaf is no longer. Instead, think tender, juicy, umami beef ribboned with greens and complemented by notes of caramelized onions. You can swap in ground turkey, pork, bison, or chicken—any ground meat will do. I used to serve mashed potatoes with my meat loaf, but once we changed to a spicy roasted cauliflower, we haven't turned back.

For the meat loaf

1½ teaspoons olive oil

½ yellow onion, diced

1 bunch collard greens

¼ teaspoon salt, plus more as needed

1 pound ground beef

1 tablespoon Dijon mustard, plus 1 teaspoon, divided

1 tablespoon ketchup, plus 1 teaspoon, divided

1 tablespoon maple syrup

1½ teaspoons balsamic vinegar

1½ teaspoons tamari

1 large egg

To make the meat loaf

1. Preheat the oven to 350°F. Line a baking sheet with parchment paper.

2. In a medium skillet, heat the oil over medium heat. Add the onion and collard greens with a pinch of salt. Cook for about 10 minutes, or until the onion is caramelized. Remove from the heat. Set aside to cool.

3. In a large mixing bowl, combine the beef, cooled onion and collard greens, 1 tablespoon of mustard, 1 tablespoon of ketchup, the maple syrup, vinegar, tamari, egg, bread crumbs, and salt. Season with pepper. Mix until just combined. Be careful not to overmix.

4. Dump the meat mixture onto the prepared baking sheet, and gently form an oval loaf, making a slight dent in the center, which will help the center cook as quickly as the edges of the loaf.

½ cup panko
    bread crumbs
    (or gluten-free
    bread crumbs)
Freshly ground
    black pepper

For the cauliflower

1 head cauliflower,
    broken into florets
1½ teaspoons
    avocado oil
¼ teaspoon salt
¼ teaspoon chili powder
Pinch ground cumin
Pinch paprika

5. In a small mixing bowl, mix together the remaining 1 teaspoon of mustard and 1 teaspoon of ketchup. Brush over the top and sides of the loaf.

To make the cauliflower

6. In a separate large mixing bowl, combine the cauliflower, oil, salt, chili powder, cumin, and paprika. Toss until coated, and scatter on the same baking sheet as the meat loaf, leaving plenty of room so the florets will roast and get some color, rather than steam. Transfer the baking sheet to the oven, and bake for 30 minutes.

7. Stir the cauliflower, and rotate the baking sheet. Bake for 15 to 20 minutes, or until the cauliflower is fork-tender and takes on a bit of color. Remove from the oven.

Mix it up: When serving a dish without lots of color variety, I like to dress it up with a light green salad or lots of chopped fresh herbs. Parsley, thyme, basil, sage, or all of the above would add a delicious pop of color for this dish. Just sprinkle on top of your meat loaf, and serve.

Per Serving Calories: 371; Total Fat: 15g; Saturated Fat: 5g; Sodium: 844mg; Carbohydrates: 27g; Fiber: 6g; Sugars: 7g; Protein: 30g

---

DIVIDE & CONQUER:
Partner 1 can take care of steps 1 and 2 while partner 2 follows steps 3 through 5 to pull together the meat loaf. Partner 1 can then jump ahead to step 6 and get to work on the cauliflower.

Sesame Beef and Broccoli with Red Pepper Rice

DAIRY-FREE, GLUTEN-FREE, NUT-FREE

Serves 2 / Prep time: 10 minutes / Cook time: 30 minutes

If you love takeout beef and broccoli, try your hand at making it yourselves. A simpler version of the classic late-night delivery dish accompanied by a flavorful rice will surely scratch that itch. I love basmati rice in any recipe that calls for rice. It has a distinctive toasty and floral aroma and cooks quickly. It may not be a classic pairing with beef and broccoli, but it's a match in my book.

1½ teaspoons avocado oil

¼ cup chopped red bell pepper

⅔ cup basmati rice

Salt

2 cups water, plus 2 tablespoons

1 tablespoon sesame oil

½ yellow onion, sliced

½ teaspoon minced garlic

½ teaspoon minced ginger

6 ounces beef tenderloin, cut into strips

¼ cup tamari

2 tablespoons maple syrup

1 teaspoon cornstarch

1. In a large skillet, heat the avocado oil over medium heat. Add the red bell pepper. Sauté for 2 to 3 minutes, or until browned and tender. Add the rice and a large pinch of salt. Cover with 2 cups of water. Cover the skillet with a tight-fitting lid, and let the rice simmer and steam for about 15 minutes, or until tender. Remove from the heat. Pile the rice into a serving dish.

2. In the same skillet, heat the sesame oil over medium-high heat. Add the onion, garlic, and ginger. Sauté for 3 to 4 minutes. Turn up the heat slightly, and add the beef. Cook for 2 to 3 minutes, or until browned. Stir in the tamari and maple syrup.

3. In a small bowl, mix the cornstarch with 2 tablespoons of water to make a smooth paste, then add it to the skillet.

Pinch red pepper flakes

1 head broccoli, broken into florets

1½ teaspoons sesame seeds

4. Add the red pepper flakes and broccoli. Cover with a fitted lid, and cook for 5 to 6 minutes, or until the broccoli is fork-tender. Remove from the heat. Serve on top of the rice, and sprinkle with the sesame seeds.

Swap it out: No need to break the bank with beef tenderloin; thinly sliced sirloin steak is not only more cost effective but also more traditional for this dish.

Per Serving Calories: 639; Total Fat: 18g; Saturated Fat: 4g; Sodium: 2,147mg; Carbohydrates: 86g; Fiber: 11g; Sugars: 20g; Protein: 37g

---

DIVIDE & CONQUER:

Partner 1 can prepare the rice in step 1 and partner 2 can take over at step 2. While partner 2 is engaged with step 2, partner 1 can quickly mix up the cornstarch and water as directed in step 3. Partner 2 can complete step 4.

Farro Risotto with Garlic-Basil Shrimp

Serves 2 / **Prep time:** 10 minutes / **Cook time:** 25 to 30 minutes

Nutty, hearty, and very satisfying, farro is the ancient grain that you walk right on by in the grocery store, because it's situated next to about 189 other odd grain types in the dry goods aisle. Couscous, freekeh, quinoa, Arborio rice, jasmine rice, wild rice, basmati rice . . . you get the picture. I love a good hearty grain, and to me, farro takes the cake. Semi-pearled farro is what you are looking for if you want to avoid the overnight soaking. I love the size and the chew of this grain and how perfect it is for a "farrotto," in lieu of a classic risotto.

3 teaspoons salted
   butter, divided
1 cup semi-pearled farro
2½ cups vegetable
   stock or water
¼ cup freshly grated
   Parmesan cheese
½ teaspoon grated
   lemon zest
Salt
Freshly ground
   black pepper
8 to 10 shrimp,
   cleaned and dried,
   tail-on okay
1 garlic clove, minced
3 or 4 fresh basil leaves,
   cut into thin ribbons

1. In a deep skillet, melt 1½ teaspoons of butter over medium heat. Add the farro. Stir for 2 to 3 minutes, or until toasted, giving off a nutty aroma.

2. Add the stock and cover. Reduce the heat so the farro is at a simmer, and cook for about 20 minutes, or until tender. Remove from the heat. Stir in the cheese, lemon zest, a few big pinches of salt, and several turns of freshly ground black pepper. Plate on a serving dish.

3. Put the skillet back over the heat, and add the remaining 1½ teaspoons of butter and the shrimp. Cook for about 1 minute, then flip, add the garlic, and cook for 1 to 2 minutes, or until the shrimp become just opaque. Remove from the heat. Pour the shrimp over the risotto, top with the basil, and serve.

Swap it out: Make this dish extra elegant by swapping out the shrimp and replacing it with a nice piece of halibut or some seared scallops.

Per Serving Calories: 504; Total Fat: 10g; Saturated Fat: 4g; Sodium: 1,014mg; Carbohydrates: 73g; Fiber: 10g; Sugars: 3g; Protein: 28g

DIVIDE & CONQUER:

Partner 1 can get the ingredients measured out and ready for partner 2 to make the risotto.

Coconut Curry Mussels

GLUTEN-FREE OPTION

Serves 2 / Prep time: 15 minutes / Cook time: 15 minutes

Mussels are one of those dishes that may seem intimidating if you have never tried your hand at preparing them. But in truth, they cook incredibly quickly, and all you really need for the most classic preparation is a little garlic, shallot, white wine (for both cooking and, of course, drinking), and some bread. And while I do enjoy mussels this way, once we tried this coconut curry version, we simply couldn't go back to the classic . . . except for the drinking the wine part.

2 pounds mussels

1 tablespoon salted butter

1 teaspoon minced shallot

1 teaspoon minced garlic

1½ teaspoons red Thai curry paste

¼ cup white wine

¼ cup tamari

1 tablespoon rice vinegar

Zest and juice of 1 lime

1 tablespoon honey

1 (13½-ounce) can full-fat coconut milk

5 fresh basil leaves, chopped

5 fresh mint leaves, chopped

Baguette, for serving (optional)

1. Clean the mussels just before use by rinsing them under cold water one at a time to gently remove any debris. The "beard" is a ropey, hairy looking bit that should be removed before cooking by swiftly tugging it off toward the hinged side of the mussel. The beard will typically come right off, but if one proves to be stubborn, simply snip it away with scissors. The mussels should all remain closed; discard any with cracked or wide-open shells. If any are just slightly open, gently tap them against the wall of your sink—they should close (if they don't, discard).

2. In a large stockpot, melt the butter over medium-high heat. Add the shallot and garlic. Sauté for 1 to 2 minutes, or until fragrant and just starting to brown. Stir in the curry paste.

3. Add the white wine, tamari, vinegar, and lime zest and juice. Stir, scraping up any brown bits from the bottom. Drizzle in the honey, and add the coconut milk (including the creamy top).

4. When the coconut milk sauce comes to a simmer, slide in all of the cleaned mussels at once, and cover with a lid. Steam the mussels for 5 minutes. Remove the lid, and stir the mussels so that the closed ones are on the bottom and the open ones are on top, then replace the lid, and cook for 2 to 3 minutes. Remove from the heat.

5. Discard any mussels that did not open. Serve by dividing the mussels between two bowls and pouring the liquid on top. Sprinkle with the basil and mint and serve with a few hunks of bread each (if using).

DIVIDE & CONQUER: *Partner 1 can clean the mussels in step 1 while partner 2 completes steps 2 and 3. After cooking, go through the mussels together to make sure they all opened.*

Cooking 101: To store mussels before cooking, remove them from the plastic bag or mesh they came in, and put in a bowl loosely covered with a damp towel. If storing a day or two before, drain off and discard any water that collects at the bottom of the bowl. Be sure the mussels smell like the ocean. Mussels should not be submerged in water when cleaning them nor should they be boiled when cooking. Instead, mussels need to steam in order to cook.

Per Serving Calories: 1,273; Total Fat: 61g; Saturated Fat: 38g; Sodium: 3,920mg; Carbohydrates: 52g; Fiber: 1g; Sugars: 13g; Protein: 115g

Parchment Fish with Summer Squash

GLUTEN-FREE, NUT-FREE

Serves 2 / Prep time: 15 minutes / Cook time: 12 minutes, plus 4 minutes to rest

The simple elegance of a self-contained fish dish such as this is wildly satis-fying. Sure, it is essentially just a piece of fish cooked in a bag—but it really is elegant, especially if you call it by its true name, fish en papillote, *which simply means "fish enveloped in paper."*

You can serve it right in the pouch. Classic flavors of white wine and shallot are always spot on with a firm white fish. If you aren't fans of thyme, try out tarragon, dill, or parsley.

1 zucchini

1 yellow summer squash

Salt

Freshly ground
   black pepper

1 teaspoon minced
   shallot, divided

2 teaspoons white
   wine, divided

2 (8-ounce) sole, cod, or
   snapper fillets

2 teaspoons salted
   butter or olive
   oil, divided

2 lemon slices

2 fresh thyme sprigs

1. Preheat the oven to 400°F.

2. Cut the zucchini and squash into 2-inch lengths. Then, trim off the outside edges of each piece so that the 2-inch pieces are square, instead of round. Next, cut in half lengthwise so that you have roughly ¼-inch slabs. Rotate 90 degrees, and cut in half again lengthwise so you end up with roughly ¼-by-¼-by-2-inch batons.

3. Cut two 12-inch lengths of parchment paper. Working with one sheet at a time, fold the parchment paper in half and crease, then lay back out flat.

4. In the center of one half, lay a large bundle of the yellow squash and zucchini batons. Season with salt and pepper. Sprinkle on ½ teaspoon of shallot and 1 teaspoon of wine.

5. Top the nest of batons with 1 fillet and a sprinkle of salt. Add 1 teaspoon of butter on top of the fillet, 1 lemon slice, and 1 thyme sprig.

6. Fold the other half of the parchment paper over the fish, tightly rolling together the edges and leaving the center puffed. The objective is to seal the parchment paper into a steam pouch for the fish and vegetables. Put the pouch on a baking sheet, and repeat the process to complete a second parchment paper pouch.

7. Transfer the baking sheet with both pouches to the oven, and bake for 12 minutes. Remove from the oven. Let sit for 3 to 4 minutes, then serve by opening up the pouch and eating immediately.

DIVIDE & CONQUER: *Partner 1 can take on steps 1 through 3 while partner 2 gathers the remaining ingredients. Together, assemble the pouches according to the directions in steps 4 through 6.*

Swap it out: In the spring, try using asparagus instead of summer squash and zucchini (and skip step 2).

Per Serving Calories: 307; Total Fat: 6g; Saturated Fat: 3g; Sodium: 224mg; Carbohydrates: 8g; Fiber: 3g; Sugars: 4g; Protein: 53g

Whiskey-Cinnamon Bananas Foster

COMFORT FOOD, GLUTEN-FREE, NUT-FREE, VEGETARIAN, VEGAN OPTION

Serves 2 / Prep time: 5 minutes / Cook time: 5 minutes

This is my husband's favorite dessert. The flavors of slightly burnt caramel and cinnamon-y salty bananas over ice cream, not to mention the flambé effect from igniting the whiskey, are simply delightful. To flambé may seem intimidating, and you're not wrong, it is fire. But aside from dramatic effect, it also adds flavor complexity, so it is a step worth taking. Once you get the hang of it (use a long-handled lighter and tie your hair back), you will want to flambé all dang day.

1 tablespoon salted butter (or coconut oil)

2 bananas

¼ teaspoon cinnamon

Salt

¼ cup maple syrup

2 tablespoons whiskey

Vanilla ice cream (or dairy-free ice cream)

1. In a large, deep skillet with a long handle, melt the butter over medium heat.

2. Cut the bananas into ¼-inch slices, and add them to the skillet. Cook for 3 to 4 minutes, or until brown, then flip them over. Sprinkle with the cinnamon and a large pinch of salt. Add the maple syrup, and simmer for about 1 minute.

3. Have the whiskey measured out and ready to go so it can be poured in all at once, and have a long-handled lighter ready. *Never* pour the whiskey straight from the bottle, because the lit fumes can funnel back into the bottle. Pour the whiskey in and then let the flame of your lighter quickly touch the liquid. Stand back, be prepared for a large flame, and keep your face away. Give the skillet a little shake and let the fire burn out, which will take anywhere from 3 to 15 seconds. Remove from the heat.

4. Scoop the ice cream into dishes, and pour the bananas on top. Serve immediately.

Swap it out: Try pineapple and brown sugar instead of bananas and maple syrup.

> ## DIVIDE & CONQUER:
> *Partner 1 can do steps 1, 2, and 3 while partner 2 stands by with the fire extinguisher and their eyebrows intact.*

Salted Maple and Apple Crisp

**COMFORT FOOD, GLUTEN-FREE OPTION,
NUT-FREE, VEGAN OPTION**

Serves 4 / **Prep time:** 10 minutes / **Cook time:** 1 hour

This homey favorite can be enjoyed with a spoon while you hover, impatiently waiting for it to cool, or dolled up and doled out with a scoop of vanilla ice cream or whipped cream. It is sweet enough for dessert and guilt-free enough for breakfast. If you like salted caramel, give this maple version a whirl.

For the filling

3 or 4 apples, any kind
½ lemon
½ cup maple syrup

For the topping

8 tablespoons (1 stick)
  salted butter (or
  coconut oil)
1 cup rolled oats
  (or gluten-free
  rolled oats)
½ cup all-purpose flour
  (or gluten-free flour)
½ cup brown sugar
½ teaspoon salt
½ teaspoon cinnamon
¼ cup maple syrup

To make the filling

1. Preheat the oven to 350°F.

2. Chop the apples into ½-inch chunks, with or without the peel (both ways are great). Put in a large mixing bowl. Squeeze the lemon over the apples to keep them from browning. Arrange the apple chunks in an even layer in the bottom of a 9-by-13-by-2-inch baking dish. Drizzle the maple syrup on top.

To make the topping

3. In a small saucepan, melt the butter over low heat.

4. In a large bowl (you can use the lemon-treated apple bowl), combine the oats, flour, sugar, salt, and cinnamon. Use a fork or whisk to stir the dry ingredients together to distribute all the flavors evenly. Drizzle in the melted butter and maple syrup. Use your clean hands to work the mixture together until it looks like wet sand.

5. Pack the crumble topping on top of the layer of apples, covering them. Transfer the baking dish to the oven, and bake for 1 hour, or until the apples are soft and the topping is golden. Remove from the oven.

Mix it up: If, for some reason, you and your partner have leftovers of this crisp, try making them into overnight oats (see page 22).

Per Serving Calories: 626; Total Fat: 25g; Saturated Fat: 15g; Sodium: 467mg; Carbohydrates: 109g; Fiber: 6g; Sugars: 68g; Protein: 5g

DIVIDE & CONQUER:
Partner 1 can complete steps 1 and 2, chopping and sweetening the apples while partner 2 completes steps 3, 4, and 5, making the crumble topping and assembling the crisp.

CHAPTER 6

Sauces & Staples

Apple Cider Vinaigrette

DAIRY-FREE, GLUTEN-FREE, NUT-FREE, VEGAN

Makes about ¾ cup / Prep time: 5 minutes

This vinaigrette is delicious on simple green salads, arugula, endive, fennel—the list goes on. Light, bright, and sweet with a slight pucker, it will become your favorite staple in no time. Honey could easily replace the maple syrup.

1 teaspoon
   Dijon mustard
¼ cup apple
   cider vinegar
1½ teaspoons
   maple syrup
¼ cup olive oil
¼ teaspoon salt

In a jar with a tight-fitting lid, combine the mustard, vinegar, and maple syrup, and shake vigorously. Open the jar, add the olive oil and salt, and shake again very vigorously. Taste, and adjust the seasoning, if needed. You can keep the dressing in the jar with the lid on in the refrigerator for up to 2 weeks.

Mix it up: Add a touch of whole-grain mustard and some minced shallot to include a bit more complexity in this vinaigrette.

Per Serving (¼ cup) Calories: 170; Total Fat: 18g; Saturated Fat: 2g; Sodium: 234mg; Carbohydrates: 2g; Fiber: 0g; Sugars: 2g; Protein: 0g

Arugula-Pecan Pesto

DAIRY-FREE, GLUTEN-FREE, VEGAN

Makes about 1 cup / Prep time: 5 minutes

Classic pesto is made with basil, pine nuts, Parmesan, garlic, lemon, and olive oil—and yes, it is amazing, but we like to change it up every once in a while. And so this arugula-pecan version came to be, to which we are equally addicted. We enjoy this pesto on eggs, pasta, rice, fish, toast, pork, burgers, and I could go on, but I will stop there.

2 cups packed arugula

2 garlic cloves

½ cup pecans

Juice of ½ lemon, plus more as needed

¼ cup olive oil

¼ teaspoon salt, plus more as needed

1. Put the arugula and garlic in a food processor. Pulse until broken down into a fine chop. Add the pecans and lemon juice. Pulse again while streaming in the olive oil.

2. Add the salt. Taste, and adjust the seasoning by adding more salt or lemon, if needed. If a smoother or thinner pesto is desired, add water a tablespoon at a time and pulse again to adjust the texture.

3. You can keep the pesto in a jar with the lid on in the refrigerator for 4 to 5 days, or you can freeze it for up to 3 months.

Mix it up: Try blending the pesto with 2 tablespoons of water and an extra pinch of salt super smooth in a blender in lieu of the food processor to use as a marinade for pork or chicken.

Per Serving (¼ cup) Calories: 219; Total Fat: 23g; Saturated Fat: 3g; Sodium: 148mg; Carbohydrates: 3g; Fiber: 2g; Sugars: 1g; Protein: 2g

House Hummus

Makes about 1 cup / Prep time: 5 minutes

Hummus has earned its place in the top 10 as far as snacks go. It's creamy, delicious, nutritious, naturally allergen-free (the popular ones, anyway), and enjoyed by just about everyone. Put your own spin on your "house special hummus" by adding extra garlic, chili, or herbs—start with this recipe and then go wild.

2 garlic cloves, minced

1 (15-ounce) can chick-peas, drained

1 tablespoon tahini

½ teaspoon salt

¼ teaspoon ground coriander

¼ teaspoon ground cumin

Juice of 2 lemons

¼ cup olive oil

¼ cup cold water, divided

1. Put the garlic, chickpeas, tahini, salt, coriander, and cumin in a food processor. Pulse until everything is chopped very finely and well combined.

2. Turn on the processor, and stream in the lemon juice and olive oil, adding 1 tablespoon at a time of water until the desired texture is achieved. I tend to use upward of ¼ cup of water because we like a very smooth and almost pourable consistency.

3. You can keep the hummus in a jar with the lid on in the refrigerator for 4 to 5 days, or you can freeze it for up to 3 months.

Swap it out: You can make hummus out of just about anything, including white beans, carrots, and even butternut squash. Replace the chickpeas with an equal amount of the ingredient you wish to swap in.

Per Serving (¼ cup) Calories: 246; Total Fat: 17g; Saturated Fat: 2g; Sodium: 584mg; Carbohydrates: 19g; Fiber: 6g; Sugars: 2g; Protein: 6g

Quickie Hollandaise Sauce

GLUTEN-FREE, NUT-FREE, VEGETARIAN

Makes about 1 cup / Prep time: 5 minutes / **Cook time:** 5 minutes

Silky, rich, lemony, salty, hollandaise sauce is basically heaven on earth. But why wait until the weekend to enjoy this exceptional condiment? With this quickie blender hollandaise, there are no reservations and no wait times—just you, your sweetie, a couple of poached eggs, and a dreamy restaurant-worthy sauce.

10 tablespoons salted butter

3 large egg yolks

1 tablespoon freshly squeezed lemon juice, plus more as needed

¼ teaspoon salt, plus more as needed

1. In a medium skillet, melt the butter over medium-low heat.

2. While the butter is melting, in a blender, combine the egg yolks, lemon juice, and salt. Blend for a minute or so, or until smooth and light yellow.

3. When the butter is just bubbling and hot, turn the blender on to the lowest setting, and slowly stream the butter into the blender. The sauce should be thick and glossy. Taste, and adjust the lemon and salt, if needed. Use immediately.

Mix it up: Try replacing the lemon juice with lime juice and adding a pinch of chili powder for a bright and spicy change.

Per Serving (¼ cup) Calories: 297; Total Fat: 32g; Saturated Fat: 20g; Sodium: 357mg; Carbohydrates: 1g; Fiber: 0g; Sugars: <1g; Protein: 2g

Asian-Style Barbecue Sauce

DAIRY-FREE, GLUTEN-FREE, NUT-FREE, VEGETARIAN

Makes 2 cups / **Prep time:** 5 minutes / **Cook time:** 30 minutes

Barbecue sauce can be an art, with several ingredients and hours of simmering. There are barbecue sauce purists out there with some incredible sauces, and this recipe is not for them. You can throw this together to use when you grill chicken, burgers, or vegetables like mushrooms and zucchini. Let it simmer on the stove while you sip your imported ale and enjoy not slaving over a 40-ingredient barbecue sauce.

1 cup ketchup

½ cup honey

⅓ cup Dijon mustard

⅓ cup tamari

¼ cup balsamic vinegar

1. In a medium saucepan, combine the ketchup, honey, mustard, tamari, and balsamic vinegar. Whisk together over medium heat until bubbles start to appear on the surface.

2. Reduce the heat to low. Gently simmer for 20 to 30 minutes, or until reduced by about a quarter. Remove from the heat. You can keep the sauce in a jar with the lid on in the refrigerator for 7 to 10 days, or you can freeze it for up to 6 months.

Cooking 101: To simmer means to cook just below the boiling point. When you set out to reduce something, you're concentrating the flavor as well as thickening your sauce.

Per Serving (¼ cup) Calories: 126; Total Fat: 0g; Saturated Fat: 0g; Sodium: 1,227mg; Carbohydrates: 29g; Fiber: <1g; Sugars: 18g; Protein: 1g

Honey-Balsamic Reduction

DAIRY-FREE, GLUTEN-FREE, NUT-FREE, VEGETARIAN

Makes about ¾ cup / Cook time: 15 minutes

I stopped buying bottles of reduced balsamic vinegar at the store years ago when I realized I could make it at home in no time and for less money. We like to buy a giant bottle of midrange balsamic vinegar and reduce the whole bottle at once. We drizzle the reduction sauce on pizza, bread, eggs, tomatoes, avocados, mozzarella, salads, and pastas. It has earned a solid place on our condiments shelf.

1 cup balsamic vinegar
2 tablespoons honey

In a small saucepan, bring the vinegar and honey to a simmer over medium heat. Cook for 15 minutes, or until the mixture can thickly coat the back of a spoon. Remove from the heat. Let cool slightly before jarring or bottling, and wait until it has cooled to room temperature before using. This can be stored at room temperature indefinitely.

Mix it up: Try making a fancy white balsamic reduction by following the same exact recipe—just with white balsamic vinegar instead of the standard version.

Per Serving (¼ cup) Calories: 85; Total Fat: 0g; Saturated Fat: 0g; Sodium: 27mg; Carbohydrates: 22g; Fiber: 0g; Sugars: 12g; Protein: 0g

Chimichurri

DAIRY-FREE, GLUTEN-FREE, NUT-FREE, VEGAN

Serves 4 / Prep time: 10 minutes

My partner would probably drink chimichurri if given the chance. For this, we thank our great friends Gretchen and Gordon, who came to visit us when we lived in Bow-Edison, Washington, for some Pacific Northwest food culture. Gordon happens to be a chef as well and treated us with an evening of grilled steaks accompanied by this herby, peppery green sauce. Now, everyone has a riff on chimichurri, but my husband just about chugged chef Gordon's signature version. Full-on green teeth and grinning with delight when he was done, as he had found the condiment of his dreams. Thanks, Gordon!

1 cup fresh parsley
    leaves (a little stem
    is okay)
1 cup fresh
    oregano leaves
½ small red onion, diced
2 garlic cloves, chopped
½ teaspoon red
    pepper flakes
¼ cup red-wine vinegar
¼ cup olive oil
1 teaspoon salt
Freshly ground
    black pepper

Put the parsley, oregano, onion, garlic, red pepper flakes, and vinegar in a food processor. Stream in the olive oil while pulsing, scraping down the sides of the bowl, if needed. Season generously with the salt and pepper. You can keep the sauce in a jar with the lid on in the refrigerator for 4 to 5 days, or you can freeze it for up to 3 months.

Mix it up: There is also a red version of chimichurri where red peppers and tomatoes can be added. Simply swap out the red onion for a white one, cut the amount of fresh herbs in half, replacing them with equal parts regular or sun-dried tomatoes and red bell pepper, and add ¼ teaspoon paprika.

Per Serving Calories: 136; Total Fat: 14g; Saturated Fat: 2g; Sodium: 599mg; Carbohydrates: 3g; Fiber: 1g; Sugars: 1g; Protein: 1g

Avocado Green Goddess Dip

DAIRY-FREE, GLUTEN-FREE, VEGAN

Makes 1½ cups / Prep time: 10 minutes

Green goddess dressing typically has mayonnaise, sour cream, anchovies, tarragon, and chervil and is very tasty. I was in need of a dip for a party vegetable tray and could not decide between a green goddess dip or the always crowd-pleasing guacamole. While I wrestled with these options, I was already going through the motions of adding a perfectly ripe avocado to the blender along with some lime juice, herbs, and garlic. A few adjustments later, we have Avocado Green Goddess Dip. We love it.

1 avocado, peeled
   and pitted
Juice of 1 lemon
Juice of 1 lime
5 fresh basil leaves
1 garlic clove
¼ cup shelled pistachios
¼ cup olive oil
¼ cup water
½ teaspoon salt

Put the avocado, lemon juice, lime juice, basil, garlic, and pistachios in a blender. Turn the blender on the lowest setting, and stream in the olive oil and water, if needed. Season with the salt. You can keep the dressing in a jar with the lid on in the refrigerator for 3 to 4 days. Freezing is not recommended.

Ingredient tip: To check to see if an avocado is ripe, take a peek under the stem. If it is mostly green, you have the best chance of your avocado being ripe, or close to it, whereas if it is mostly brown, then the avocado is already past its prime.

Per Serving (2 tablespoons) Calories: 80; Total Fat: 8g; Saturated Fat: 1g; Sodium: 114mg; Carbohydrates: 3g; Fiber: 1g; Sugars: <1g; Protein: 1g

What's for Dinner?

Sometimes, deciding what to make for dinner is the hardest part. Perhaps you are jonesing for something sweet, or you feel like having breakfast for dinner, or you have a hankering for some seafood. Explore the recipes in this book by going with your gut and following your cravings. Cook what you feel like having tonight. If you're not constrained by time, ingredients, or cooking method, use this list to find your next favorite.

I feel like making . . .

CHICKEN:

Almond and Parmesan Chicken with Maple-Dijon Dip (page 76)

Chicken Marsala with Mushrooms Two Ways (page 78)

Panfried Chicken with Hot Honey (page 114)

Skillet Sherry Chicken Thighs and Maple-Orange Roasted Roots (page 152)

Chicken Paprikash (page 155)

Roasted Chicken over Peasant Bread with Fingerlings (aka Million-Dollar Chicken) (page 157)

BEEF/PORK/LAMB:

Peach, Prosciutto, Rocket, and Burrata Salad (page 36)

Cannellini Bean and Bacon Succotash with Arugula (page 83)

Spaghetti Carbonara (page 81)

Lamb on a Stick with Wilted Spinach (page 85)

Puff Pastry Eggs with Prosciutto and Cheese (page 138)

Cheesy Sausage and Tomato Frittata (page 134)

Beef Cabbage Rolls in Creamy Tomato Sauce (page 116)

Skillet Steak and Potatoes with Crispy Sage and Red Wine (page 119)

Stuffed Meat Loaf with Spicy Roasted Cauliflower (page 162)

Hoisin Pork Lettuce Cups with Savory Carrot Slaw (page 160)

Sesame Beef and Broccoli with Red Pepper Rice (page 164)

SOMETHING FROM THE SEA:

Chili-Lime Shrimp Salad (page 70)

Caesar Salad with Fried Kale and Pine Nuts (page 66)

Panfried Thai Curry Wild Salmon Cakes (page 91)

Old Bay Butter Shrimp and Corn Polenta (page 87)

Maple-Dijon Salmon with Greens Beans and Caramelized Shallot (page 93)

Pecan Butter Halibut and Roasted Broccoli (page 89)

Coconut Curry Mussels (page 168)

Farro Risotto with Garlic-Basil Shrimp (page 166)

Parchment Fish with Summer Squash (page 170)

Dill Cucumber Noodles with Smoked Salmon (page 32)

SOMETHING VEGETARIAN:

See Index, page 194

BREAKFAST:

Chocolate-Cherry Granola Bars (page 26)

Chocolate Chia Pudding Pots (page 24)

continued >>

Caesar Salad with Fried Kale and Pine Nuts (page 66)

Panzanella Salad with Radicchio, Asiago, and Olives (page 68)

SOME LIGHTER FARE:

Smoky Tomato-Lentil Stew (page 144)

Thai Curry Butternut Squash Soup (page 148)

Arugula Salad with Roasted Grapes and Walnut Dressing (page 106)

Cream of Zucchini Soup with Cumin and Coriander (page 140)

Broccoli, Tart Cherry, and Pecan Slaw with Poppy Seed Dressing (page 39)

Cilantro-Lime Cabbage Slaw with Ginger-Cashew Dressing (page 41)

Crunchy Thai-Style Veggie Noodle Salad with Peanut Sauce (page 34)

Dill Cucumber Noodles with Smoked Salmon (page 32)

SOMETHING SWEET:

Chocolate-Cherry Granola Bars (page 26)

Chocolate Chia Pudding Pots (page 24)

Cinnamon, Apple, and Almond Butter Overnight Oats (page 22)

Nutella and Strawberry Fool (page 43)

Probably Your Grandmother's Cookies and Cream Icebox Cake (page 45)

Sweet Balsamic Berries and Vanilla Bean Cream (page 47)

Cranberry-Coconut Granola (page 54)

Lemon Ricotta Pancakes with Blueberry Butter Syrup (page 58)

Cinnamon Granola Berry Parfaits (page 56)

continued »

WHAT'S FOR DINNER? *continued*

Brown Butter Crispy Rice Treats (page 95)

Panna Cotta with Roasted Strawberries (page 121)

Banana Crème Brûlée (page 123)

Chocolate Croissant Bread Pudding (page 125)

Red Berry Marbled Macaroons (page 127)

Dark Chocolate–Covered Strawberries (page 129)

Whiskey-Cinnamon Bananas Foster (page 172)

Salted Maple and Apple Crisp (page 174)

SOMETHING WITH CHOCOLATE:

Chocolate-Cherry Granola Bars (page 26)

Chocolate Chia Pudding Pots (page 24)

Nutella and Strawberry Fool (page 43)

Probably Your Grandmother's Cookies and Cream Icebox Cake (page 45)

Chocolate Croissant Bread Pudding (page 125)

Dark Chocolate–Covered Strawberries (page 129)

A STARTER OR A SIDE DISH:

Savory Peach and Melon Gazpacho with Feta (page 30)

Dill Cucumber Noodles with Smoked Salmon (page 32)

Crunchy Thai-Style Veggie Noodle Salad with Peanut Sauce (page 34)

Peach, Prosciutto, Rocket, and Burrata Salad (page 36)

Whipped Feta and Spiced Honey Schmear (page 28)

Broccoli, Tart Cherry, and Pecan Slaw with Poppy Seed Dressing (page 39)

Cilantro-Lime Cabbage Slaw with Ginger-Cashew Dressing (page 41)

Caesar Salad with Fried Kale and Pine Nuts (page 66)

Panzanella Salad with Radicchio, Asiago, and Olives (page 68)

Cannellini Bean and Bacon Succotash with Arugula (page 83)

Sweet Potato Fries with Garlic-Basil Aïoli (page 102)

Blue Cheese and Scallion Scones (page 100)

Arugula Salad with Roasted Grapes and Walnut Dressing (page 106)

Walnut-Tarragon Stuffed Mushrooms (page 112)

Harissa and Honey-Roasted Carrots (page 104)

Smoky Tomato-Lentil Stew (page 144)

Cream of Zucchini Soup with Cumin and Coriander (page 140)

Corn and Crab Chowder (page 142)

Thai Curry Butternut Squash Soup (page 148)

OR, OF COURSE, SOMETHING WITH BACON:

Peach, Prosciutto, Rocket, and Burrata Salad (page 36)

Cannellini Bean and Bacon Succotash with Arugula (page 83)

Spaghetti Carbonara (page 81)

Puff Pastry Eggs with Prosciutto and Cheese (page 138)

MEASUREMENT CONVERSIONS

OVEN TEMPERATURES

FAHRENHEIT	CELSIUS (APPROXIMATE)
250°F	120°C
300°F	150°C
325°F	165°C
350°F	180°C
375°F	190°C
400°F	200°C
425°F	220°C
450°F	230°C

WEIGHT EQUIVALENTS

US STANDARD	METRIC (APPROXIMATE)
½ ounce	15 g
1 ounce	30 g
2 ounces	60 g
4 ounces	115 g
8 ounces	225 g
12 ounces	340 g
16 ounces or 1 pound	455 g

VOLUME EQUIVALENTS (LIQUID)

US STANDARD	US STANDARD (OUNCES)	METRIC (APPROXIMATE)
2 tablespoons	1 fl. oz.	30 mL
¼ cup	2 fl. oz.	60 mL
½ cup	4 fl. oz.	120 mL
1 cup	8 fl. oz.	240 mL
1½ cups	12 fl. oz.	355 mL
2 cups or 1 pint	16 fl. oz.	475 mL
4 cups or 1 quart	32 fl. oz.	1 L
1 gallon	128 fl. oz.	4 L

VOLUME EQUIVALENTS (DRY)

US STANDARD	METRIC (APPROXIMATE)
⅛ teaspoon	0.5 mL
¼ teaspoon	1 mL
½ teaspoon	2 mL
¾ teaspoon	4 mL
1 teaspoon	5 mL
1 tablespoon	15 mL
¼ cup	59 mL
⅓ cup	79 mL
½ cup	118 mL
⅔ cup	156 mL
¾ cup	177 mL
1 cup	235 mL
2 cups or 1 pint	475 mL
3 cups	700 mL
4 cups or 1 quart	1 L

INDEX

D

O

P

W

Z

ACKNOWLEDGMENTS

Thank you to my love, my partner, my husband, my baby daddy, Casey Rigney—thank you for loving food like I do. Thank you for all of the time you gave me to myself to write this book while you kept things afloat. To my mom, Shelly Ross, thank you for being the tree that this apple (that's me, I'm the apple) rolled from, for all of the wonderful things you have cooked for me throughout my life, and for being my culinary touchstone. To Simone Garreau, thank you for always being my great supporter and just naturally offering encouragement at all the right times. I love our dining adventures together; it is the most fun to eat with you. To Adrienne Cook Garreau, a true inspiration in the kitchen and the most fun to talk shop with. Last but not least, to my editor, Bridget Fitzgerald, and the Callisto Media team, your timely and graceful guidance for this first book of mine has been a wonderful experience. I have been inspired by all of you. Thank you all from the bottom of my always-hungry heart.

ABOUT THE AUTHOR

Ryan Ross is a Virginia native and has been in the realm of bespoke dining as a culinary producer, consultant, and a private chef for the last ten years. She grew up in her mother's organic health food store, attended culinary school in New York City, and furthered her farm-to-table studies in Washington State. She has traveled around the world writing menus and training chefs in local and seasonal food fare. Ryan is the creator of Lovage and Company, curated culinary creations for plant-rich, wild, and seasonal happenings, including large-format feasts in uncommon spaces and collaborative dinner parties with local farms, vineyards, and breweries. She has been featured on two episodes as a co-host of *Scraps* on A&E as well as a winner of the *Chopped* episode "Light Makes Right." Ryan currently lives in Virginia with her husband and daughter, where she continues her dinner-partying adventures in collaboration with local farms, preparing seasonal menus. Find her on Instagram at @thechefryanross.

CPSIA information can be obtained
at www.ICGtesting.com
Printed in the USA
LVHW051313080820
662282LV00002B/4